Working Successfully with Screwed-Up People

Books by Elizabeth B. Brown

Living Successfully with Screwed-Up People
Surviving the Loss of a Child
The Joy Choice

Working Successfully

with

Screwed-Up

People

Elizabeth B. Brown

Revell

a division of Baker Publishing Group
Grand Rapids, Michigan

Published by Revell
a division of Baker Publishing Group
P.O. Box 6287, Grand Rapids, MI 49516-6287
www.revellbooks.com

Printed in the United States of America

Library of Congress Cataloging-in-Publication Data
Brown, Elizabeth B.
    Working successfully with screwed-up people / Elizabeth B. Brown.
        p.   cm.
    Includes bibliographical references.
    ISBN 978-0-8007-2011-7 (pbk.)
    1. Psychology, Industrial. 2. Interpersonal relations. 3. Interpersonal
relations—Religious aspects—Christianity. 4. Interpersonal conflict.
5. Employees—Psychology. 6. Personnel management—Psychological aspects.
I. Title.
HF5548.8.B6894 2012
650.1′3—dc23   2011051194

To protect the privacy of those who have shared their stories with the author, some details and names have been changed.

The internet addresses, email addresses, and phone numbers in this book are accurate at the time of publication. They are provided only as a resource; Baker Publishing Group does not endorse them or vouch for their content or permanence.

12   13   14   15   16   17   18   7   6   5   4   3

This book is dedicated to Richard Bowie, Doug and Amy Williams, Tom and Nancy Carter, and my husband Paul. Running a family business together has increased my appreciation for the gifts each of you bring to the company table. How fortunate to be friends, as well as family!

Contents

Acknowledgments

How is it possible to name all the people who have contributed to this book? Real life lessons come through people, those with whom you live, work, share, struggle, and laugh. To my family: no one has more reason to appreciate the gift of *you* than me. To my friends, I say with heartfelt emotion: thank you for being a friend—and for all your advice that has given meat for this book! To those with whom I have worked: I have learned both *what to do* and *what not to do* from you. Thank you for both! To those with whom I have partnered in a successful endeavor: you taught me much! To those with whom I have royally blown it: your grace has helped me learn lessons, instead of load myself with guilt. To my publishing family: gratitude has not enough words!

1

Working Successfully
with Screwed-Up People

It doesn't take two people to change a relationship;
it takes one.

Working *Successfully with Screwed-Up People* is not like any other business book on the market. It is a workers' manual, how-to book, management guide, and co-worker's Bible. You won't find rules for growing the business, staying afloat, or finance's bottom line here. This book deals with the "driving me crazy" people issues that, nine times out of ten, you carry home at night—the gnat issues that come with working with a (pardon the expression) "screwed-up" person: the co-worker in the next office who chats more than she works; the off-the-wall supervisor; the customer who, by the way, isn't always right; and the endless list of nail-biters, naggers, hangers-on, bullies, and incompetent, irresponsible co-workers and customers. This book deals with an unspoken, rarely addressed, and universal problem: getting along with those in your work world.

You aren't alone if you think the people with whom you work are making your job more difficult. We all have someone with whom we deal (or have dealt) who aggravates and irritates. Perhaps you will appreciate the comment made by a middle-aged man shuffling behind me with his bags at the Salt Lake City airport. All flights to the East Coast were canceled due to snow and ice. Airline customer service was in crisis. My guess is that you have experienced such a maze, where strangers become instant friends, commiserating about the unanticipated nightmare.

This baggage-pushing chap's loud pronouncement turned a lot of heads: "I'd choose to stand in line any day if it would get me out of the office."

I responded, "Wow—must not be much fun at your job." He laughed, and quickly justified his remark, saying, "Standing in airport lines is a walk in the park compared to dealing with the crackpots I work with."

This man definitely had a "working with screwed-up people" problem. There is trouble in the corral if standing in an airport line is more palatable than returning to your office.

Have you noticed at-work problems are addressed as challenges to be met, dealt with, and resolved? People problems, on the other hand, like those of Scott, the man in the airport line, are stuffed under the table, whispered about, and often utilized as excuses for poor job performance. The "sort of joking" comments we make about our work environments that are the tip of the iceberg of people problems is the meat upon which *Working Successfully with Screwed-Up People* will chew. Though this book isn't written about management, supervision, team playing, or even customer satisfaction, it is all about business. So often these hinted-at negative interactions at work clog up the gears of business. Improve work-place relationship interplay, and the practical business side will run more smoothly. Jobs are as much about the undisclosed problems and opportunities of in-terpersonal relationships as work skills.

Maybe Scott stumbled into working with "crackpots" because, like most of us, he accepted his job when a door opened for employment. He didn't choose the people with whom he worked. He chose a way to earn money for food and rent. Perhaps his job description has him plowing someone else's cornfield without the possibil-ity of planting his own garden. Perhaps he was fortunate to find the career of his dreams. Either way, it is safe to say no one told Scott that signing his job contract included a shotgun marriage to a family of strangers.

> *J*obs are as much about the un-disclosed problems and opportunities of interpersonal relationships as work skills.

This book is for all of us who need tactics to free us from spin-ning around the "underwear issues," the ones no one shares except through innuendo, gossip, and raised eyebrows at work. We can be encouraged by practical ways to deal with irritating people problems that can cause us to roll our eyes and force us to stuff our true feelings. We can learn keys that unlock positive ways to release stress and use humor as we respond to bang-your-head-against-the-wall aggravating behaviors. *Working Successfully with Screwed-Up People* may keep you from twisting around the person you find offensive or, in Scott's case, preferring a three-hour rescheduling line at an airport to being in the office.

Scott is certainly not unique. Michael, a local flower guru, is passionate about his floral business. His creative juices flow with the seasonal changes. He loves his career, even though his stories of challenges make you wonder why he finds it enjoyable. He chuckles about the Godzilla mothers-of-the-bride, is flabbergasted by customers who want to return flower arrangements because dinner parties were canceled at the last moment, and is blown away by those who insist on the impossible.

You can choose—choose to be unflappable, imperturbable, and unflustered!

"Sometimes I laugh, but my patience has a short life. I need help! What can I do to keep my mouth shut when I am dealing with a jerk or someone with ridiculous expectations? For example, just before closing time on Valentine's Day, Mr. Bigwig came in, huffing 'Got to have some roses . . . three dozen, hurry.' I certainly recognized a man in crisis, but not only were the roses gone, almost every other type of flower was too. I showed the distraught guy what I had available, but nothing suited. He wanted roses and he wanted them now. Finally, tired of being nice, I let it out: 'Sorry, late-to-the-party Larry, we don't have what you want. Next time try to make your plans a little earlier.'"

Michael acknowledged that his off-the-cuff comment wasn't customer friendly. He wanted advice on ways to cool down and become dispassionate when his buttons were hot. Perhaps, like Michael, you need help in addressing with calm and self-control the unreasonable expectations of a difficult person. *Working Successfully with Screwed-Up People* will help you stop muddling through unreasonable expectations, spinning off negative comments, or losing personal control with people who choose their modus operandi to manipulate things their way. The person who is exasperating, difficult, offensive, uncooperative, and unreasonable *chooses* his behavior. You, also, can *choose*—choose to be unflappable, imperturbable, and unflustered!

Remember the story of the little engine that had to climb the big mountain with a very heavy load, too heavy for such a small engine? The other engines taunted him. "You are too small. Your engine was made for straight roads. We are the big dogs. Give up." The little engine felt wimpy and underpowered as he started the journey. *Surely*, he thought, *I can do it if the others can*. He began to repeat over and over, "I think I can, I think I can, I think I can." Moving forward required gigantic effort. It felt impossible. He chugged and pulled, heaving as he carried his load over the mountains and through the woods to its destination. He started his journey believing his size determined his ability. He arrived at his destination with a paradigm change.

You may need a paradigm change to meet your challenging people problems at work. You need insight that boosts your resolve to handle fitful, hurtful, or unjust behavior. Could a thought really change any of your work problems? After all, life isn't a fairy tale. You aren't a train engine. But, like the small engine, you can harness your somersaulting emotions by simple focus. Thoughts direct how we act and react.

The first book I wrote in this series was *Living Successfully with Screwed-Up People*. It has been an international bestseller, picked up by readers just like you in bookstores, airports, grocery stores, and Walmarts. You will probably agree with me that issues at home and in the workplace are somewhat the same. After all, people are people and we all respond best to the same things: respect, appreciation, and care. But no one believes we handle our home family in quite the same way as our work family. We can disconnect from our work family, keep them somewhat at a distance, and are not as blown out of the water by issues that threaten one of our co-workers. At work, someone's problems, even though they may affect us, are still *his* problems. We may be willing to help, but we certainly are not going to carry the same feeling of responsibility we would if it were our spouse or child.

re insights about relationships that will help you through
or the inevitable storms that threaten your home in *Living Successfully with Screwed-Up People* and your work in *Working Successfully with Screwed-Up People*. You can be happy and satisfied in the midst of overwhelming responsibilities, conflicts, and even difficult relationships if you look at the situation from a new, healthier perspective. Begin fresh today to change any self-defeating behaviors that hold you hostage. The work world may be full of screwed-up people, but your world no longer has to revolve around them.

It takes only one person to change a relationship.

- Take back the power from the difficult people in your life.
- Respond productively when confronted.
- Remain poised and in control when everyone around you loses it.
- Win fairly in unfair battles.

My question for you is simple: *Do you really want to bring about positive change in your negative relationships at work?* If so, you must be willing to change first. Unless you change, it is unlikely your relationships will do anything but sink deeper into distress. Change causes surprise. Those around you ask, "Why are you so different?" It is impossible to continue the same type of interaction if one of the parties has metamorphosed his or her actions and responses. It doesn't take two people to change a negative relationship; it takes only one! That's a hope point!

So your workplace is not perfect? Put on your glasses. You are about to see a world of possibilities, a way for you to be free from the webs that screwed-up people spin, and a way to find peace in a significant portion of your life—your job! And in the process you'll find a treasure: an inner strength and confidence forged through the uncomfortable life lessons gleaned from dealing with difficult people.

Let's start by remembering these insights.

Insights

- Jobs are as much about the undisclosed problems and opportunities of interpersonal relationships as work skills.
- It doesn't take two people to change a relationship; it takes one.
- You can choose to be unflappable, imperturbable, and unflustered.

Questions

1. Are you finding someone at work difficult?
2. Do you consider the people you work with as family?
3. How many hours do you spend with your co-workers?
4. How many hours do you spend with those outside of work, not counting sleep time?

2

Who Is the Problem?

*Get up high enough and step back far enough to see
the whole picture.*

There is a degree of shrewdness you need before entering the
workforce, and often no one tells you any of the necessary
skills to obtain that wisdom. Why is that? Why are there no courses
to teach essential people skills before you join the ranks of the
employed? I know your parents and friends eagerly congratulated
you on finding a job, especially in this job market. Did the more
experienced share with you what to expect from your work family, or did they merely smile knowingly and ask what your job
entailed? I'm sure they were thinking, *Why say anything now? He
will learn on the job.*

Were you adequately prepared, or did you feel like a babe when
you walked through the company door? One young woman told
me she understood the job particulars of "where to be when," but

had no idea how to handle the role tiers at her job. What should she call her boss: Mr. Smith or Joe? Should she speak up in the conference room or defer to the white hair? Was she expected to share new ideas or submit to the wisdom of her supervisor, who was too old to ease into the newest technology? Should she pal with co-workers, or consider anyone in the company poison outside the office doors?

Figuring out how to maneuver in the social field of the workplace is critical to job satisfaction. Most of us are surprised by the number of people who simply walk away from a decent position because they don't like someone: one out of six, with as many as one out of three stressed to the breaking point by the negative attitudes or actions of fellow workers according to the 2001 Harris poll.[1] Maybe others who, like most of us, were not advised on how to handle the ingratiating, fawning, or uncompromising behavior on their team stay in the job by slinking into a cubicle, hoping to be out of the target zone. The good news is that it is never too early or too late in your career to learn people skills that make work life more pleasurable.

Lauren, a computer technician struggling with co-worker issues, felt mired in a swamp of emotional muck. "I'm in quicksand," she said. "How do you work with someone who ignores, demeans, questions, or rejects you? How do you deal with mean and unfair behavior? How do you go the second mile when that merely means being taken advantage of? How do you keep your job when you are blamed for someone else's messes? I'm afraid of a misstep, terrified I will blurt out the wrong idea or blunder into a wrong action."

Lauren is in a great place! Whatever action she takes offers her the opportunity to grow wiser. Difficult people are very effective at getting what they want because their actions intimidate or compel. Thinking about how she could make her actions positive would arm Lauren for future encounters. Knowing there is no one right solution to dealing with her problems frees her from thinking of a blundered attempt to resolve the thorny issues as a failure. Instead, it becomes a lesson of what didn't work. Eventually, if you continue to respond as a mature adult, not allowing the other person's actions to put you in a pickle, his tactics will change. Why? Because what he is doing to get his way is not working.

Change begets change.

Figuring It Out

The first response to irregular actions is surprise, then anger or hurt, guilt, and questioning. You wonder: Is the person really that difficult, or are you just being overly sensitive? Is what you are asked to do really unreasonable, or merely a different way to get the job done? Were you simply put off by the manner or quirkiness of your co-worker's personality? You must step back for an objective look. That may sound simple, but if it were, a book like this would not be needed. Most of us are bewildered by the difficult people problems at work. We don't know how to work with curmudgeons, cranks, loony tunes, whiners, or narcissists.

I suggested to Lauren that she needed an aerial perspective to figure out who was the problem. Lauren understood, telling me, "I always feel lost in NYC, an ant in the midst of skyscrapers, traffic, and people everywhere, with streets in all directions. But when I am looking at the city from above, it is easier to put it in perspective."

Relationships need the same type of aerial view. You can't figure out whether you are the problem or if the blame belongs to the other guy if you are stuck in the middle of the fray. Just as when we wander amidst skyscrapers, in relationship quagmires we are on the ground—stuck between emotions, stung by out-of-the-blue encounters, wondering if we are the cause, and questioning what we should do to make things better. In the middle of that chaos we must corral our emotions, whip them into shape, and react with objectivity. It becomes even more difficult to distance yourself if you bring your home problems to work, where they piggyback onto co-worker problems. Leave personal problems at home so when you step into the workplace you deal with only work issues. There are enough of those to keep you busy.

Wrong actions are wrong; wrong responses to wrong actions are equally wrong.

Stepping back to gain some objectivity about the situation begins your journey out of your emotional maze. You may come to the conclusion your negative reactions are unwarranted, or you may affirm that your discernment hit the target: you are dealing with a jerk. The good news is discerning who is the problem frees you from swirling emotions. But you are not off the hook: you are part of a team. It is crucial to mature your skills at peacefully working with those whose burrs irritate.

Aerial vision clears away illusion. Wrong actions are wrong; wrong responses to wrong actions are equally wrong. Aerial vision gives you an objective perspective by which you can determine:

- The possibilities
- The improbabilities
- The impossibilities

The Yardstick Measurement

If you are objective and view a difficult relationship as if you are an outsider, you will often find that your judgment is far more rigid and unforgiving for some than for others. Differing yardstick measurements are why you can find the capriciousness of a certain co-worker or acquaintance entertaining, while the same behavior in someone else is a potential earthquake. "There's a woman in my office who is so off-the-wall that she makes me cringe, then chuckle with laughter," Lauren said. "I really like her but I am glad she isn't on my team. Her sarcasm and mouthy put-downs are far more out in left field than those of the woman who pushes my buttons."

Perhaps, like Lauren, you will recognize it is more than just behavior that triggers your negative reactions. Think carefully about why you feel smothered, angry, frustrated, or hurt by someone—and yet similar behavior in another is dismissed without more than a glancing thought. You can grow to appreciate—even enjoy—the person whose capriciousness and idiosyncrasies currently irritate if you refuse to allow her behavior to get under your skin. If you burrow in the muck, you become an integral part of the problem, and it is no longer just the other person's behavior that is wrong and causing turmoil.

Turning a toxic relationship into a healthy one requires hard work, objectivity, and *laughter*. Humor opens our eyes to see baffling issues in a new, more detached way. Suddenly you are looking at the problem without the consuming emotion. You let the screwed-up person own her behavior, instead of carrying it on your shoulders or adding credibility by responding. Humor prevents you from being jolted by every challenge like a wagon without springs. It is a life preserver when you start to sink into a swamp of chaos. If you laugh instead of wallow or rage, irritation and resentments slip away and a sunny spirit takes their place.

The Hiccups

The problem is *hiccups*. A teacher shared a hiccup experience she had in her first year of teaching. She was barely getting her bearings when the principal called her to his office for a private conference. The principal asked, "Do you have anything to tell me?" She was dumbfounded. What did he want to know? What had she done? After she squirmed sufficiently, he said, "You are pregnant!" In the 1970s, being pregnant was enough reason to lose your job. She wasn't pregnant, and blurted out something like, "I guess time will tell," and left. This teacher, now a principal, assured me that she learned a lot by that assault. But still, for all of us, surprise attacks, or hiccups, are unanticipated and hard to prepare for.

The teacher squirmed because she felt bushwhacked. If she had been older and wiser in the screwed-up people department, she might have laughed and brushed off the rudeness, maybe saying something like, "Sorry. Bet you thought you would see me squirm with that statement!" Or she might even have had the power to say straight out, "How immature, unprofessional, and rude to make such a suggestion in this manner." Maturity and experience help you assess and assert yourself when someone is intentionally cruel or uses a warped sense of humor to hurt. Still, you and I know that there is plenty we put up with at work because we don't want to lose our jobs!

There is plenty we put up with at work because we don't want to lose our jobs.

Lauren empathized with this teacher. The times that hung her up at work were also hiccup moments that stymied her by surprise. She didn't know how to respond or what to do. I suggested Lauren collect her thoughts and trust her instincts. If she left conversations bewildered, stung, disbelieving, and wondering if the person meant what she said, something was wrong. When something feels off-base, it probably is.

Lauren needed a few simple, noncommittal statements in her verbal arsenal to keep from appearing defensive or flustered, so she could fly above the fray when another encounter reared its head, statements such as: "I need a moment to think about this." "Interesting. I'll consider that." "Is that what you think would be best?" "How would you have done this differently?" "I'm sorry. I'm trying to do my job without worrying about that problem."

Or perhaps Lauren needed merely to laugh and brush off the suggestion or remark as if it were absolutely absurd or made in jest. Refusing to give off-the-cuff wrongs or ridiculousness the power of emotion simply lets them bounce off you like water off a duck's back.

Surprise attacks are like hiccups: unanticipated.

Let's review the steps to developing an aerial vantage point:

- Step back to gain perspective when you confront people problems at work.

- Lower your natural defenses so you can analyze who the problem is.

- Put away naiveté. When something feels off-base, it probably is.

- Determine your course of action.

- Arm yourself with a verbal arsenal of positive, noncommittal comments and actions to stop negative flow.

Relationships that are screwed-up cause a lot of pain. If you are just beginning to twist, now is the time to reverse your patterns. It will take far less work now than if you wait until later. If you have already hit bottom in a relationship at work, and are lost in a quagmire that costs you time and emotional energy, you can reverse the patterns. Often it takes hitting bottom to shatter the naive thoughts that everyone will like you or that you will like everyone.

Low points can be hope points.

It is possible to regain control of your thoughts and restructure the relationships that have tumbled into chaos at work by stepping back and assessing your situation, getting up high enough to see the whole picture. Then, regardless of others' actions, you are responsible for rising above the wrongs to do the right. Take heart. Low points can be hope points.

Insights

- An aerial perspective helps you through the maze of challenges in difficult relationships.
- Wrong actions are wrong; wrong responses to wrong actions are equally wrong.
- Surprise attacks are like hiccups: unanticipated.
- When something feels off-base, it probably is.
- Low points are hope points.
- Laughter helps you fly above the idiosyncrasies or atrocious behavior of another.

Questions

1. Are you struggling with someone at work?
2. What are the signs that you are spinning off your interactions with the person?
3. Why do you react so strongly against this person when another co-worker with many of the same personality traits is a friend?
4. What could you do to keep from feeling irritated, hurt, angry, or guilty?

3

Hardwired

Preprogrammed and Unchangeable!

> In the workplace there are enough targets without aiming at each other.

Five words started our phone conversation: "Help! Our ship is sinking!" As Jack, an executive in a midsized company, explained his problem, it became abundantly clear that something needed to change or else the company ship might truly sink. That was the bad news. The good news was that the very thing threatening to sink his company was also one of the most necessary tools for large-scale business growth. Jack just didn't know it yet.

Once at the company's headquarters, I began to see the source of the tension in this business: partners who read "how-to" from different books. "Jack worries about everything," Lori, his partner, said with a sigh. "It's like I see the business world from 40,000 feet, and he is on the ground counting the boulders that stand in the way of our success."

The source of this tension, extremely divergent viewpoints, is in reality a great source of hope for the business's success. The problem is that though it may be true that two heads are better than one, it does not *feel* better. I was hopeful that as we discussed the value of "different," each partner could begin to appreciate the unique gifts the other brought to the table.

There were two teams working in this business: Jack's and Lori's. Jack knew the ins and outs of the business, having headed it for years. He studies the bottom line and safeguards details in a daily diary. He arrives on time to work and stays well beyond the required workday, analyzing the financials and possible pitfalls of the business in order to be prepared for any downturns. He prefers to store up his nuts for the winter in preparation for a blizzard. Jack is nonconfrontational in negotiation, feeling the facts should speak for themselves. Like a Boy Scout, his motto is "Be prepared," especially in a down economy. Jack is challenged by his partner's seeming optimistic disregard of the facts and figures.

> *Two merging into one may be weaker than two working side by side, but it feels better.*

Lori handles the entrepreneurial aspects of the business. She's a visionary. She looks at the big picture, considers the facts, but believes all will be well, because "it always is," and is sure business would show up at the door in time for the next payable bank note. She enjoys going out on the limb to be fair or to entice clients. She prefers long lunches with clients to strengthen relationships, as opposed to clocking in on time at the office. She believes it takes money to make money. Hiring the best people out there may cost more, but in the long run would save the company. Lori was challenged by Jack's fact-based judgment.

It is in this tension that the hope of the company's success lives. Jack and Lori's very different leadership styles and perspectives painted a broad-brushed picture in board meetings. Some members of the board affirmed Jack's conservative, hunker-down stance, especially in the down economy. Others on the board supported Lori in her thought that this was the ideal time to move forward with plans, before loan interest went up and everyone else was vying for the same customer base. The way their board handled the situation was by majority vote after much protracted discussion. Easy? Absolutely not!

Could two such opposite approaches within the same company be good for business? Of course. It scopes the whole picture—but wow! It causes major stress! The way we think and the way we judge create immense problems in "getting along" issues. The business becomes a war zone if respect is not the cornerstone upon which such differences in a company are laid. I thought it wise to meet with the company board and executive staff to give them two concepts to drink in:

1. *Not everyone needs to be the point guard.* The coach of every great basketball team counts on a team composed of a variety of players: point guard, shooting guard, small forward, power forward, and center. Each player has a honed skill that builds the team and one goal: winning. Does this seem obvious? Then why do we attempt to make everyone play from the same position in business?

2. *Celebrate the differences.* We are hardwired differently. If Jack sees the downside of the economy and Lori sees the possibilities of investment at the same time, together they can help the board evaluate the best moves for the company to survive and thrive.

Breaking Down the Barriers

I knew the company's board and staff needed insight in order to appreciate the ideas of others who seemed to be flying on different planes. It is normal and natural, when we encounter someone who staunchly believes something we *know* is wrong and may force us into a wrong direction, to growl as our antennae go up and our body armor locks on.

We are not programmed to see the world through someone else's eyes. Nature has hardwired our operating system: the core of each of us, the unchangeable and individual ways we interpret our world and react to it. Those traits are prepackaged and wired to the side of the coin from which we perceive, interpret, and judge information. It even sets the best time for us to be online (time cycle), the structure in which we feel most secure (clutter vs. order), our background screen (noise or quiet), and the way we recharge our power (alone or with others).

We label this encoding "temperament." It is part of nature's protective and inflexible pathway to help us circle the wagons. You see the world white; I see it black. You work best in the evening; I'm on fire in the morning. I need my downtime alone to recharge; you are on a perpetual people-fest to energize. Together we have a full-circle perspective.

Animal species protect themselves through coloration that blends with the environment, replaceable limbs, repugnant odors, or menacing-looking body armor. For humans our protection is mind-directed. We outthink our enemies and survive in dangerous situations by analyzing our options. By joining forces with someone who sees a different side of the puzzle, we develop keener insights for our survival.

Some even argue that temperament is our instinctive behavior, somewhat like how a dog turns in circles before he lies down or flocks of birds migrate. Perhaps that is stretching the line, but as I talked to Lori, she commented, "My kids certainly came with their own ways of acting. One is quiet and loves to do her own thing; my other was born *smoking cigars*. I certainly influence the way they act out, but I haven't changed that basic personality I noticed from day one."

Understanding Our Hardwiring

The most critical points for any of us to remember about personality are simple:

1. Key personality traits are unchangeable.
2. The way we express these traits is malleable.

Temperament traits can be arranged in a scale of opposites. For instance, an easily identifiable pair of opposite temperament traits is that of orderliness and disorderliness. Jack's office was simple and clutter-free. Lori's seemed a perfect model of disarray. Lori quickly piped up in defense of her clutter, declaring that she knew where everything in her office was, and having it all in sight made her feel in control of her world. Jack laughed. "Clutter makes me feel out of control," he said. "I would label myself a one for order, and Lori a ten for disorder."

> *Nature has hardwired your operating system— the core of you.*

Labels, however, are misnomers for identification. Extremes have their place in business success. Being at either end of the scale does not make you screwed-up, though it may seem so to someone whose traits differ from yours. Alexander Graham Bell, the eminent scientist, inventor, engineer, and innovator who is credited with inventing the first practical telephone and a multitude of nineteenth-century wonders, was a ten in the time cycle of night and day alertness. He stayed up all night doing experiments, then catnapped during the day. Do you think his wife thought his sleep pattern normal and healthy?

In the following chapter, we will delve more deeply into the opposing traits of personality, and then follow with a chapter on ways to appreciate and handle differences in temperament with grace. It is normal to be less reactive—and in better self-control—when we do not perceive differences as personal challenges.

As a teaser, let me list ten questions that may help you recognize traits of personality that are unlikely to change over the course of your life. Perhaps, like Jack and Lori, you will have an immediate flash of insight and new appreciation for simple characteristics that previously seemed threatening and distracting.

1. Do you prefer to ask questions and seek advice before making a decision, or do you prefer to think through the issue on your own in order to evaluate the opinions of others against your own internal compass?
2. Do you make decisions based on facts or on feelings?
3. Do you base your decision on what is best for you and/or your company, or what is best for everyone involved?
4. Do you prefer to work in a quiet environment or surrounded by music or other workplace sounds?
5. Do you prefer an uncluttered environment or one that is filled to capacity or even overflowing?
6. Are you more alert in the morning hours or nighttime hours?
7. Do you feel safer with firmly set rules or flexible rules that act as guidelines?
8. Do you see the cup half full or half empty?

9. Do you reenergize by being with people or by being alone?

10. Do you set work guidelines and then trust that the task will be completed satisfactorily and on time, or do you prefer to check up on progress after making the assignment?

Divergent perspectives are either a safety net or a battleground. The difference between the two is the level of respect for differences. The greater the understanding and appreciation, the more co-workers temper their tension, drumbeating, and battling against the immutable, and instead seek to rationally find what can be changed, what may be changed, and what will not change. Simply stated, we discern when:

- Agreement or compromise is likely.
- Agreement or compromise is possible.
- Agreement or compromise is not possible.

Forging Unions through Tension

Science describes nature as being in a constant state of tension. We recognize that productive relationships are forged by the union of uniquely different forces: the sun and moon light the day and night, electrons and neutrons generate electricity, acid works with alkali for digestion, fine motor coordination is the product of two opposing muscle groups. Tension *works*.

How interesting, then, that even though we affirm differences and acknowledge their reality in nature, we tend to demand conformity when it comes to how the people around us deal with problems. Different is fine—as long as it doesn't invade our inner circles or mess with the way we get our job done. That's why we affirm and bond with those who think and react as we do. If "different" works beside us, we label him as an outsider and keep him on the fringe instead of making him a valued, full-fledged member of the work tribe. How sad! Different can enrich our worldview, broaden our outlook, and increase the possible ways to work outside our box. The good news: recognizing that diversity is the wellspring of survival in nature and in business may keep your emotions from surging. *You are who you are* as far as temperament is concerned. Count that a good thing!

Insights

- Nature has hardwired your operating system: the core of you.
- Temperament is the impervious and immutable path through which we interpret our world.
- We are not programmed to see the world through someone else's eyes.
- The most critical thing to know about personality is which traits can be influenced toward change and which cannot.
- You are who you are!
- Two merging into one may be weaker than two working side by side, but it feels better.
- The way we gather information, think, and judge create immense problems in the "get along" arenas!

Questions

1. Answer the questions in this chapter that help to identify temperament traits. Make a list of yours.
2. Think of someone with whom you work who is extremely irksome. Make a list of their temperament traits.

3. Is it their temperament or their behavior that you find irritating?
4. What are some ways you might share your perspective with others whose basic temperament differs from yours—without their becoming defensive?

4

Temperament's Nuts and Bolts

The more I understand who I am, the better I can appreciate who you are.

Most of us in business study personality in order to focus on necessary skills for company growth. We participate in seminars that identify us as lions or lambs, profile us as introverts and extroverts, and help us build our appreciation for different approaches. Still, I daresay that few of us appreciate some of the subtle ways innate characteristics of temperament interplay. We appreciate and understand traits similar to our own; we even recognize how our own strengths can bolster or be helped by a co-worker's disparate characteristics, but an irksome majority of dissimilar traits can cause us to identify the individual as obstinate, ludicrous, or downright ignorant. When I told him this, Jack laughed. "My bubbly assistant certainly has me pegged," he said. "She brings me coffee from Starbucks each morning and keeps her perkiness under wraps until I move from slow-go to high speed."

As we talked it became obvious a simple session with Jack and Lori's staff to identify the unchangeable might eliminate much of the frustration that was causing negative undercurrents in their company. No matter how many times a morning person gives perk-up advice to a slow-starting co-worker, his or her body's wake-up time will not change. Being as wise as Jack's assistant, who provides caffeine and quiet rather than chatter and a to-do list, is easier when we consciously identify our innate personas. In the following chart I will single out ten traits. Perhaps, as you think about the points of stress you experience with a co-worker, you will think of other characteristics. Temperament traits are the "who we are" of personality. They are the drivers of our rationale and actions. They in no way excuse hurtful, unjust, or discourteous behavior, but they will determine how we see and interact with our world—no question.

Again, remember that temperament, unlike behavior, is immutable. The temperament you are born with is the temperament you will die with, unless you have a life-changing experience like the character Ebenezer Scrooge in Dickens's *The Christmas Carol*, who was visited by ghosts from his past. Jack and I discussed a friend of his who literally seemed to be a new man after having a near-death experience. That happens, but as we will see in the next chapter, perhaps his changes were behavioral or the result of new priorities—how he acted, not his temperament.

It is possible to override your natural tendencies, or at least temper them. For instance, you may see the cup half empty by design, but you are tired of looking at the downside of life. You determine to express only positive thoughts. Over time, you will be able to modulate by conscious effort your pessimistic temperament trait

Key Temperament Traits

1. **Time Cycle**
   - **Morning:** I am more alert in the morning and run down as the day progresses.
   - **Night:** I am slow to awaken and as the day progresses feel more and more alert.

2. **Environment A**
   - **Order:** I work better when everything is in its proper place.
   - **Disorder:** I work better when surrounded.

3. **Environment B**
   - **Quiet:** I want my surroundings quiet when I am working or concentrating.
   - **Sound Around:** I work best with music or other noise in the background.

4. **Reenergizing**
   - **Extrovert:** Too much time alone depresses me.
   - **Introvert:** I need "me" time. I become depressed if I can't have time to myself.

5. **Fact Finding**
   - **External Thinker:** I love to debate, question, and think out loud.
   - **Internal Thinker:** I process my information internally, think it through, and respond to others after I draw my own conclusions.

6. **Focus**
   - **Self-centered:** If I don't look out for myself, no one else will.
   - **Other-centered:** Let's work together. We need to help each other.

7. **Judging A**
   - **Fact Based:** I want the facts, concrete information upon which to base my decisions.
   - **Emotion Based:** I trust hunches, body language, and feelings.

8. **Judging B**
   - **Optimism:** I'll handle problems if they come, but why should I worry about what may never happen?
   - **Pessimism:** I focus on the problems so I am not caught unawares.

9. **Structure**
   - **Rule Follower:** The best thing in the long run is to follow the rules, no exceptions.
   - **Rule Guide:** Rules are meant to be guides, not to block common sense.

10. **Actions**
    - **Laid-back:** I'm happy for you to do what you want on your own schedule—me too!
    - **Compulsive:** I need to check to make sure we are all doing it right and on time.

that, unlike your behavior, is preset. I recalled the story of my left-handed grandmother. As a child, her teachers tied her left hand, forcing her to write with her right hand. She learned the skill, but that did not change her predilection, only her behavior.

I asked Jack if understanding his employees' temperaments might affect how he worked with his staff. "An easy place for me to be intentional is an employee's time cycle, hiring morning people for the early jobs and saving the late evening jobs for people whose mental acuity turns on at night. If most of the staff doesn't come to life until later in the day, why meet at eight a.m. to conference?"

Lori piped in about temperament traits affecting environment. "I am a sound-around person, but my husband turns off the music as soon as he gets home, which drives me crazy. He says he thinks better without the music. As I thought about it, I believe I think better with music in the background. Not only has knowledge of the temperament traits opened my eyes to some of our issues at home, it's made me far more aware of how these traits affect us at work. I've always been bothered that Jack shuts his door at the office. It makes me hesitant to bother him when I need help. Maybe he, like my husband, thinks more clearly without music or extraneous office noise. It has nothing to do with his desire to help, just his wiring."

> **P**essimists prepare for the squalls, and optimists find rainbows in the storms.

"I was surprised that we might be preprogrammed with the optimism/pessimism trait," said Jack, nodding. "I am uncomfortable that I tend to see the cup half empty when that is perceived as a negative trait, yet I think it's critical to keep watch that the cup doesn't become dry. I thought people like Lori, who have a brighter, 'it's all going to work out' attitude, were just being unrealistic.

Maybe pessimists prepare for the squalls, and optimists find rainbows in the storms."

A few traits put employees at diametrical positions with no easy way to reconcile conflicting views. The more extreme you are in one of the traits, the more naturally defensive you will be of your position. For instance, people who are other-focused and always put people before profits simply cannot tolerate the me-centered folks' emphasis on the bottom line. Yet, those on the "what's in it for me" side consider people with such an attitude to be naive bleeding hearts, and think, *How can a successful business's main focus be what's good for the other guy?* Such opposing viewpoints may be mediated by rationale, but most often the ultimate decision will be made by the big dog or the majority vote. Knowing when to quit fighting a done deal is critical to getting along with others in our business world.

Rule followers cannot tolerate those who use rules as mere guides. For example, I remember discussing a legal case in Manassas, Virginia, where a five-year-old boy kissed a little girl in his class at recess. He was suspended and required to take sexual harassment training before being allowed back in the classroom because of the school's No Tolerance policy. Those who followed the rules acknowledged it was a bit extreme, but agreed that in the long run exceptions to a rule caused havoc. Others countered their logic, saying, "Where is your common sense?"

Those who base their decisions on facts do not necessarily "think better" than those who trust their intuitive feelings. Studies show that both temperaments make equally good decisions. The way one comes to a decision is a natural tendency, not an ability. Similarly, those who prefer to determine choices by how they feel do not necessarily have better emotional reactions. The two divergent pathways of thinking are just that: divergent. So, how do you handle such discordant paths of thought? Carefully. Explain your thoughts, arguments, and justifications. Then back off.

Internal thinkers and external thinkers may be offended by the way thoughts are expressed in discussions. An internal thinker may believe external thinkers butt in, question, debate, and counterargue as if in a boxing bout. An external thinker may believe internal thinkers are sheep following the thoughts of others, hesitant to have their own opinions and afraid to think outside the box. Some may consider those who listen to others before talking as having keener insight, while at the same time thinking those who speak up quickly are better leaders.

How might these traits play out in meetings? I asked Jack what he might do to support natural tendencies and yet make his conference time more productive. He listed several ideas:

- Pass out agendas prior to the meeting.
- Talk about the differences in discussion styles of internal vs. external thinkers.
- Help the internal thinkers pause, back up, and reenter the conversation rather than be stymied if their conversation was interrupted, and continue forward without becoming defensive.
- Affirm the depth of thought brought to the table by internal thinkers.
- Affirm the right of external thinkers to think out loud and change their argument after considering the discussion, as long as they do not interrupt or dominate the interchange of thoughts.
- Help external thinkers appreciate the quieter style of internal thinkers, and likewise help internal thinkers understand the way external thinkers process their thoughts.

- Help everyone recognize that both types of thinkers can be strong, effective leaders.

Business has multiple difficult issues that heat up the emotions and create diametrically opposing arguments. Balanced thinking is critical to consider the long-term consequences. Understanding the value of different points of view and respecting the right of each to argue his thoughts ultimately brings about the most acceptable compromise for the moment, even if there is no solution acceptable to everyone. If the resolution is found to not work, the tension pot will keep bubbling. It becomes crucial to consider changing tactics.

For instance, though it is desirable to serve everyone of any age with state-of-art medical care, replacement parts, and transplants, doing so is not possible in the current state of modern medicine. In the early years of the twenty-first century, many physicians across the nation closed their office doors. Medicare/Medicaid, insurance plans, necessary upgrades in technology, and additional staffing needs were driving costs to the point of no return. Business doesn't survive if there isn't enough income to make it profitable.

> *A few traits put employees at diametrical positions with no easy way to reconcile conflicting views.*

Implementing a Plan

Perhaps this "know your traits" list will help you analyze the way you and those with whom you work are programmed. Jack's staff studied the traits. Each was asked to analyze the way he or she interacted with others and come prepared to share that in the next training session. You might find this helpful not only at work, but also at home.

Appreciating our unique operating systems keeps us from banging our heads against a wall! The goal is to appreciate, respect, and utilize our differences, not try fruitlessly to change the immutable.

1. Know your traits if you are an internal thinker or work with one.

1. You want to think, analyze, and evaluate the possibilities before you give your opinion.
2. Popcorning ideas causes you to feel uncomfortable.
3. You consider it rude and belittling to be interrupted when you are explaining your thoughts.
4. You prefer an agenda before the meeting so you can think it through.
5. Being interrupted or questioned before you explain your whole rationale stops you midsentence.
6. You prefer meetings to be scheduled, not spontaneous get-togethers.

2. Know your traits if you are an external thinker or work with one.

1. You like to think with people, questioning, debating, and projecting your thoughts out loud.
2. You appear confident and aggressive because you tend to impart your ideas strongly.
3. You have no trouble changing your position after it has been debated if another position seems more tenable.
4. You are not concerned that some people rarely share their thoughts. You may even perceive that the problem is an intelligence issue that limits their ability to think outside the box.
5. You tend to be enthusiastic and full of zeal as you discuss.

44

6. You prefer to start meetings with small talk and light conversation.
7. You often jump in when others are speaking, correct, and ask questions in a strong, confident way.
8. You tend to excel in people skills, but if out of control will dominate conversation and overvalue your own opinions.

3. Know your traits if you make decisions based on feelings.

1. You trust those flashes of insight that seem to bubble up from your subconscious mind.
2. You think facts must be in balance with insight and feelings.
3. You weigh the situation to achieve balance: the greatest harmony, consensus, and fit, considering all the people involved.
4. You are keenly aware of body language.

4. Know your traits if you make decisions based on facts.

1. You trust the facts and figures.
2. You don't want to deal with hunches or possibilities.
3. You distrust hunches, theory, and abstract thinking.
4. You want business decisions to be made on what is best for the business, not what makes people feel good about the business.
5. You want the matter settled, doors shut, and projects completed.
6. Common sense sounds "emotional" to you.

5. Know your traits if your focus is self-centered or you work with someone who is.

1. You see no reason to consider the needs of others before your own.

2. Business is all about doing what needs to be done to succeed; the ends justify the means.

3. If you don't look out for yourself, no one else will.

4. You think do-gooders in business are naive.

5. Business is about winning.

6. Know your traits if your focus is other-centered or you work with someone who is.

1. You are concerned about fairness.

2. You often give up an opportunity if taking it would hurt someone else.

3. You do not understand anyone who looks out for only himself.

4. You tend to defend people.

5. You are a team player.

6. You are more concerned about the customer than the bottom line.

7. Know your traits if you use rules as a guide or work with someone who does.

1. You prefer using common sense to judging a situation by the rules.

2. You do not believe one rule is good for all situations.

3. You are willing to listen to a rule-bound person, but will override the rule every time if there seems a better, fairer, or kinder way to deal with a people problem.

4. The emotion of the problem and how it affects someone counts to you.

5. You are all about being "fair."

8. Know your traits if you are a rule follower or work with someone who is.

1. You prefer regulations, rules, and handbooks.
2. You do not believe exceptions should be made to the rules.
3. You believe the best choice in the long run is to follow the rules.
4. You will follow the rules, regardless, and work toward changing them if you think it best, but until the rules change, you uphold what is legislated.

I visited with Jack a few weeks after our training session to ask how things were going. Was their ship still sinking? He laughed, and said, "I am much more aware of how important it is to screw the right lightbulb into the right socket. But I still blow some situations royally. Last week I asked a company engineer to do a mock-up of our newest project. He told me how long it would take him to complete the task, but I thought it best to keep prodding him along. Finally, he asked if I wanted him to finish the job or if I wanted to do it myself. I got his point. My need to oversee and talk through the project was counter to his doing it on his own. I saw clearly I needed to study me as much as the other guy!"

> *Appreciating who you are is as critical as understanding the other person.*

Insights

- There is no one way of discerning or choosing that is better than another.
- We have a bit of each trait, but most people are clearly more dominant in one preference.

- The more extreme you are in one of the traits, the more naturally defensive you will be of your position.
- The only possible position with some temperament traits is "agree to disagree."
- Appreciating who you are is as critical as understanding the other person.

Questions

1. Can you identify your temperament trait in each of the ten pairs?
2. Can you identify the temperament of a difficult co-worker?
3. Are there other temperament traits that you think guide the way we interpret, judge, and act?
4. Can you share a time different temperaments caused your business to struggle?
5. How was this problem resolved?

5

My Behavior—My Choice?

Behavior is what I do, not what I think, feel, or believe.

It is easy to understand why survival depends upon the need to be curious about the environment in which we live; why mothers who are raising children need to be more verbal than fathers who are hunters and providers; and why all of us need to be capable of handling our own lives. We can even understand why nature programmed some of us to be more alert at night while some are more alert in the morning. Yet some temperament drives make you throw up your arms and cry, "What makes you act like that?!"

In the movie *Shrek*, grumpy, reclusive ogre Shrek is absolutely frustrated by Donkey, the talkative animal who loves everyone and chats it up with anyone. Shrek thinks of himself as an onion with layers. Donkey is aghast! No one should think of himself as an onion. He suggests, "You know, not everybody likes onions. What about cake? Everybody loves cake!" Shrek growls, "I don't care what everyone else likes!"

Donkey persists. "Parfaits! Have you ever met a person, you say, 'Let's get some parfaits,' they say '. . . I don't like no parfaits'? Parfaits gotta be the most delicious thing on the whole . . . planet!"[1]

Shrek is intent on projecting himself as a fiend; Donkey wants him to be likeable. Wanting someone to be something they aren't seems to be characteristic of many of us, especially when, like Donkey, we know it would be best for everyone. Donkey has a point: even ogres are responsible to behave in ways that don't drive others away.

> *Wanting someone to be something they aren't seems to be characteristic of many of us, especially when we know it would be best for everyone.*

Admittedly, Shrek has a "getting along with others" problem that causes endless trouble in the movie. We see the same in employees who cost companies tremendous amounts of time, energy, money, and frustration. Shrek couldn't do anything about his innate programming, the lens through which he interpreted his world, any more than you or your co-workers can. But he could control his behavior—and as the movie continues, he does so to win the love of Princess Fiona.

Of the people who were laid off their jobs in 2010 (excluding jobs lost from downsizing or business closings), 85 percent were let go because of personality problems.[2] They offended, affronted, disrespected, insulted, slighted, and upset others. They were not intellectually deficient; their behavior was emotionally immature, missing the keys that facilitate working amicably. The cost to both employee and employer is staggering: to replace a knowledgeable employee averages $70,000, including hiring, training, and loss of productivity, according to the Bureau of Economic Analysis.[3]

Figuring Out If We Can Change

From the beginning of recorded history, man has struggled to understand the other guy's buffaloing behavior. Stories mimicked life experience: the gods were rebellious and quick-tempered, and in battle the wicked fought with the virtuous. The ancients believed men, like the gods, were driven by body chemicals, heredity, astronomy, nature, or magic. They believed the way each of us behaved was just the way we were: set and unchangeable. If the gods had no power to change how they worked together, how was it possible for mere mortals? "You are who you are" is the wisdom of the centuries.

In the nineteenth century Austrian neurologist Sigmund Freud and Swiss psychiatrist and pastor Carl Jung questioned this assumption that behavior was unchangeable. They observed that certain characteristics of personality were inherited (nature), even as other personality traits were tempered by observation and experience in our formative years (nurture). Together nature and nurture program our subconscious. Jung and Freud contended one could override this programming by conscious directives. However, they acknowledged it takes a lot to make someone want to make the effort to bring about significant change. In the same way that writing with the left hand is hard for someone who is right-handed, so overriding subconscious drives is possible but extremely arduous. Simply said: people can change; however, significant change is unlikely—and most likely we will only change in the way we behave.

Simply said: people can change; however, significant change is unlikely—and most likely we will only change in the way we behave.

Katherine Cook Briggs, who with her daughter Isabelle Myers developed the successful Myers-Briggs Personality Profile test in the mid-1900s, studied personality to understand her son-in-law, whose actions and attitudes were so markedly different from those of her family. In order to figure out what made him *tick* when everyone else in her family *tocked*, she deliberated over psychological litera- ture and read multiple biographies. Her efforts to figure out how to cope with differing attitudes of family members resulted in an assessment test administered today to as many as two million employees annually. Her conclusion was the same as Freud and Jung: our thoughts and actions are driven by temperament, but behavior, though affected by temperament, is a choice to stay within or break free from established boundaries to get what we want.

Temperament is hardwired, but behavior is a choice.

Behavior is flexible because it has to be. That is why someone can act one way with one person and completely different with another. Such behavior is quite observable in children. For example, one parent says *do* and the child immediately *does*. The other parent says *do* and the child *does*, but only after being threatened with punishment. Behavior does whatever we will it to. That is important to understand when you are working with or evaluating an employee whose behavior is rude, angry, grating, or irksome, and is being justified by an extraneous condition. Be assured, his behavior is getting him what he wants, regardless of whether he implies differently. Look at the traits of behavior. Behavior:

- Is out front, easy to identify
- Is moldable and malleable
- Conveys and personalizes our thoughts, decisions, and emotions
- Is directed by temperament, but able to flex to cooperate with others

- Fluctuates with mood, problems, stress, and a host of extraneous influences
- Is able to camouflage motives
- May mimic expected actions to get what is needed
- Becomes the identification tag: i.e., sad, happy, aggressive, laid-back
- Is quite changeable, and yet is subject to temperament's draw to return to base characteristics

Companies offer in-house counseling services, seminars, or time off to handle such issues as anger/stress management and addiction. The goal here is to arouse our awareness that it is not only the chaos churners that need to modify their behavior, it is also those of us who may be surprised to learn that our own responses may be adding to the problem. If every time someone throws a temper tantrum you give her what she wants, you are as much a part of the unhealthy dynamic as the person who controls by anger. If you rescue the person who never finishes his work on time by pitching in to help, why should he change?

A pediatrician specializing in the care of newborns in crisis described her week of caring for multiple preemies teetering at death's door as extremely intense. Still, she was amazed that she was less tired than after the quiet workweek she spent dealing with another physician whom she found incredibly petulant and hot-tempered. She carried home her irritation and edginess. As we were talking I asked the physician why she thought the critical care issues felt less overwhelming than working with her colleague. "I have a chance to make life better for the preemies. I can't change the egomaniac!" she said.

I laughed, but suggested that she had much more power to bring about change than she voiced. Her colleague would have no choice but to change if she no longer interacted with him in the same manner. The physician countered that her number-one rule was "You can't fix crazy." But it seemed to me he might be more *cunning* than *crazy*. His behavior backed his co-workers against the wall. They preferred to do his work rather than call him for help when another pair of hands was needed. Perhaps the rule in his case would be better worded as "Figure out why someone is crazy, then stop playing their game."

*B*ehavior not only can change, it does change—when the person fails to get what he wants from what he is doing.

We will address many tactics that help us control our responses and reactions to people we consider difficult throughout this book. The physician and I did discuss her problem further, and I will give you the same advice I shared with her: if you are beating a drum, repeatedly counseling someone to change just like Donkey pleaded with Shrek, stop! The more noise you make, the more the listener closes his ears and puts up his defenses. This is the time for you to pause, as I suggested to the physician, and consider what he is gaining from his negative behavior. Plainly stated: behavior not only can change, it does change—when the person fails to get what he wants from what he is doing. Think through your actions and responses. It may not be just the other person who needs to change.

Stop the March

Jean Henri Fabre, a French naturalist in the late 1800s, spent his life observing insects and spiders. He wrote simply of what he saw in the gardens and fields near his home, compiling the information and pictures into his ten-volume *Souvenirs Entomologiques*. One of his most noted studies was on processionary caterpillars. These caterpillars follow their leader through the trees, linked head to tail in one great chain, devouring leaves as they march. Fabre placed a group of the insects on the top of a pottery crock. A world of greenery lay within inches of the crock, but the caterpillars, locked into their march, followed blindly, round and round, until days later the march ended in the death of the insects. They did not break the pattern, even though following the same-old-same-old meant death.

You may be locked into a march around screwed-up behaviors just like a processionary caterpillar, stuck in the same old ruts and grooves. If you are, don't be discouraged. Habits and patterns of behavior are not set in concrete any more than the pattern of the caterpillars' march was unchangeable. After all, just by moving the caterpillars, Fabre changed their march from the trees to the crock. They marched on, barely missing a step. Your challenge is not just to change your march's location, but to stop the march completely.[4] Thankfully, you can do it! You aren't a caterpillar.

Insights

- Understanding personality is not just about the other person; it's also about "me."
- It pays to screw each lightbulb into the right socket.
- Nature and nurture enjoin to determine our personalities.
- Simply said: people can change; however, significant change is unlikely—and most likely we will only change the way we behave.
- Temperament is hardwired, but behavior is a choice.
- It may not just be the other person who needs to do something differently.

Questions

1. Are you locked in a game with someone whose behavior is driving you bonkers?
2. If so, what do you think he or she is gaining by the behavior?
3. How can you change your interaction?
4. Think about your own behavior. What are you gaining by your actions or attitudes?

6

People Don't Want to Be Fixed

Different is the norm.

Different is the norm. In fact, on average, less than five people in any group of a hundred will think and respond like you do. So it should not surprise you that when you go to work, share your incredible idea, and pour your all into a project, it is likely that others on your team will question your plan and find flaws in your design. It's not personal. Each of us internalizes and interprets the same issue from different vantage points.

In the movie *Vantage Point*, a terrorist detonates a bomb in a jam-packed square in Spain as the crowd listens to the US president's speech. The movie replays the same scene repeatedly from the perspective of several onlookers: secret agents assigned to protect the president, an American tourist who recorded the scene, and others in the crowd. Each vehemently defends what he or she saw. Are we not the same? We work together toward the same goal at the office, but heatedly defend our own way of accomplishing the task as best. Successful business requires an *esprit de corps*. How is that possible when we seem to run on such different tracks?

Ashley was struggling with this issue. "It's politics as usual," she bemoaned. "I expected everyone to get along when I became the preschool director of a megachurch; instead, I got the same old games I had in my last school. Teachers argue, parents question, and the church staff tries to direct. I was well-trained, but no one told me this job required the tact of a career politician!"

Politics in the best sense entails the art of respect and compromise.

Ashley needed encouragement. I assured her that she was already well-trained in politics. Anyone appreciating and teaching to the uniqueness and needs of each child in a classroom is a master at respecting and encouraging *different*: different perspectives, different ways to work through problems, and different abilities. That is what politics in the best sense entails—the art of respect and compromise.

To get everyone on the same track seems almost impossible when you consider the different ways nature and nurture affect our view of work issues. Even as children we began to interpret our world through our unique temperament and experiences. For example, even the description of a common fruit by a child can depend upon when the family purchased it. A banana may be green, yellow, or if more ripe, brown. Think of how such differences multiply!

Would we be happier if we could tamper with nature to shape us all from the same cookie mold? Perhaps, but:

- We would lose the opportunity to look at problems from a different vantage point.
- We would miss the opportunity to glean wisdom and insight from a different vision.

- We would lack the stimulation channeled by being forced to consider the pros and cons.

"I recognize the advantages, but I still turn into a porcupine when someone counters what I think is best or feel is the wrong way to accomplish the task," reasoned Ashley. "I can know a supervisor believes he is right, even when I know he is wrong. I can appreciate why my co-worker has a bad attitude, but find her flaunting it and playing the victim unacceptable. What can I do to keep from bristling when *different* pokes its head into my realm?"

Different doesn't have to be wrong.

I thought Ashley had targeted the problem: we are programmed to believe what *we* do is the right way *to do*. We justify even our wrongs. Al Capone, the notorious gangster of the early 1900s, questioned why he was imprisoned. He terrorized Chicago, murdered, blackmailed, and smuggled liquor during Prohibition. Yet he didn't understand why he was targeted by the FBI. He reasoned, "It was business. I did what I had to do."

Political Advice

When encountering someone's perplexing or aggressive behavior, it may be helpful to consider several possibilities.

1. People can be clueless to what you think is obvious.

It is difficult to imagine that someone could be clueless about your expectations when you are certain you have clearly delineated your position. An attorney explained his office's rules for personal space and dress code. He laid out the law: no little doodads or obvious clutter on the desks; dress in classic work-appropriate clothes. Yet his receptionist layered her desk with family photos and knickknacks made by her children. She explained, "This isn't clutter, it's the reason I work." When clients made sly remarks about his receptionist's attire, he, again, was taken aback. How could she mistake classic dress as including a sleeveless T-shirt, no bra, and showing off enough to set off alarms? When reprimanded, she commented, "I thought summertime would be more casual." His receptionist's actions felt to the attorney like flagrant disregard for the rules.

Advice: Intentional acts need to be addressed firmly; clueless acts need to be addressed gently. The goal is to bring about necessary change in the most caring manner, not show your power by discharging your guns. Basic assumptions often differ.

2. Experience teaches that there is more than one way to effectively get the same job done.

"I can attest to that," said Ashley. "I almost killed the sale of my preschool to a teacher who was a recognized, gifted professional. The school was my baby, which I nurtured and dedicated to a creative education emphasis, growing little minds. It was acknowledged as the leading program in Boston and, thus, had a three-year admission wait list, a very good selling point. The problem was the potential buyer's philosophy of teaching was 180 degrees different than mine: she coddled and pampered. But the strange thing was, the school retained its wait list for admission after she bought it. Our very different approaches were both striving for the same goal: children who learned the joy of learning."

Advice: Keep in mind many roads lead to the same destination.

3. It is not always about me.

The past often pokes its head into the present. Many times the chill you feel from a co-worker has little to do with you. It has all to do with the other person's unresolved issues with someone from her past or tensions on the home front. Ashley, the nursery school director, was overly sensitive to church staff bickering because she had been stung by innuendo and rumors that derailed her previous job. The past weighed heavy on her shoulders. She needed to learn from her past, then leave it behind.

Advice: Brush off behavior that is offensive or bewildering.

4. It may be about me.

You may be part of the problem. People may be improperly reading your approach, your facial gestures, the way you express concern, or the way you give instructions. For instance, which comment would you most appreciate if your supervisor were expressing his concern for your work on a project?

    a. You should do it like this . . .
    b. I'll help you work through this problem . . .
    c. Call me when you get the problem worked out and we'll talk about it . . .

Whatever your preference, the other options will seem to be unnecessary interference, control, or disinterest. Yet the supervisor's goal is the same as yours: to get the job completed well. Pause when you feel reactive energy bubbling.

Advice: Evaluate carefully whether your words and actions are being interpreted correctly if you feel negative vibes from others.

61

5. Know where your responsibility ends.

Many people enter adulthood with tremendous emotional deficits and unmet needs. They are emotionally immature. They enter the workforce expecting the worst, suspicious, needy, or naive to the extreme. They may be overbearing and aggressive or draped in low self-esteem. Growing up is each individual's responsibility. Be patient. Be caring. Lend a helping hand, but not one that enables crippling behavior. Ultimately, no one is strong unless they are standing, like a table, on their own legs.

Advice: The goal at work is interdependency, not codependency.

If you are struggling with the "politics" in your job, take heart. You aren't alone. But struggling against what is normal behavior gets you nowhere. Co-workers push their own agendas because they are invested in the process—they have spent their time, energy, and thought. Instead of struggling against the inevitable, find ways to listen, understand, share, and compromise. If this is challenging for you, why not try these proven techniques:

- Suggest talking together about contentious issues.
- Explain that you would like to understand their dissimilar viewpoint and perspective.
- Listen attentively.
- Ask questions to understand, not to debate.
- When the explanations are finished, ask if you may share your thoughts.
- Seek compromise, if agreement cannot be reached.
- At the very least show respect for a contrary view to keep the doors open for future dialogue.

Goal: Understanding

Autism is a brain disorder that affects 1 out of every 110 babies born today.[1] It creates a malfunction in a person's ability to communicate, form relationships with others, and respond appropriately to the external world. The thinking patterns of individuals with autism are markedly different from the way in which "normal" people think. Would an autistic child want to think as you do? Ask Dr. Temple Grandin, an autistic woman who *thinks like a cow*.

Her parents were told she should be institutionalized. She didn't talk until she was three-and-a-half-years-old, communicating her frustration by screaming, humming, and peeping. She lived afraid. Panic attacks were everyday occurrences. She fixated on things and repeated whatever she heard. She had to wear loose-fitting clothes to counteract her repulsion to being touched, which created sensory overload. Kids thought her weird and taunted her. She felt different, alone, and disliked.

Today Dr. Grandin is listed as one of the twenty-five "2010 Heroes of *Time* Magazine." The author of the article, a professor at Harvard University, writes, "What do neurologists, cattle, and McDonald's have in common? They owe a great deal to one woman . . . Temple Grandin . . . an extraordinary source of inspiration as she has used her ideas, visions, and actions to transform the world and have a positive life-changing effect on autistic children, their parents—and all people."[2]

She tells her story of "groping her way from the far side of darkness" in her book *Emergence: Labeled Autistic*, a book that stunned the world because, until its publication, most professionals and parents assumed an autism diagnosis was virtually a death sentence to achievement or productivity in life. The *Time* article, instead, called Dr. Grandin an inspiration. She not only has a PhD in animal science and is a professor at Colorado State University, she is also a sought-after author and speaker and a foremost design engineer for animal chutes and housing. Her disability has enabled her to understand and be considered an expert on the animal mind, as well as the autistic mind.

Despite her so-labeled disability, she has stated that "if I could snap my fingers and become nonautistic I would not do so. Autism is part of who I am. I am grateful for the way I think."[3] Dr. Grandin encourages parents and teachers to focus on what a child can do, instead of what they can't do. It's no different in your work world.

No one wants to be fixed.

No one wants to be fixed. Each of us is as keen to be appreciated for who we are and valued for what we contribute as Dr. Grandin is.

The number-one factor in job satisfaction is not salary or vacation time. It is feeling appreciated by those who evaluate you, who know your work, and who see your efforts. Team spirit is strong when the team focuses on and appreciates what each member can do and what each brings to the table, not what he or she can't do.

An elderly man, hobbling to the speaker's stand with two canes to steady his gait, approached me after a grief seminar. His only child, a sixty-five-year-old son, had died from a heart attack. He and his wife were hoping to find help that could ease their grief. He shook my hand and said, "Thank you for talking about the differences between how men and women grieve. I have not understood my wife."

I was astounded. Before me was a man who had been married nearly seventy-plus years, and yet he was baffled by his wife's reaction. The good news is that he was searching for answers. He did not want to change his wife; he wanted to understand her. Sometimes we waste time trying to change what we simply must try to understand and appreciate.

Ask: Am I wanting to change this difficult person—or understand him? Bear in mind that your own resolution to succeed at getting along with your cohorts and customers is more important than any other. Attempt to work with, rather than avoid or struggle against, those who don't think and act as you do. Deal with issues in a politic manner.

1. Consider whether an action is meant to demean or harm, a personal attack, versus simply being another way to view the situation.
2. Take down your defenses; *different* may not be about you.
3. Mull over whether your actions may have armed someone to react against you personally.
4. Appreciate that *different* may expand the options.
5. Find ways to tailor approaches to meet the different needs of others; in return, you will feel empowered and partnered.
6. Know people can be clueless to what you think is obvious.
7. Recognize *different* can be right, even when it sits on both sides of the fence.

No man is ever wise by chance.

You have the opportunity to either see others as NPLU (not people like us) or to appreciate the wisdom that flows from a different vantage point. Being realistic about the unlikelihood that your ideas will be accepted as flawless has much to do with being wise. No man is ever wise by chance.

Insights

- Politics in the best sense entails the art of respect and compromise.

65

- Different is the rule, not the exception.
- Different doesn't have to be wrong.
- No man is ever wise by chance.

Questions

1. Are you able to appreciate or do you feel challenged by different ideas and work habits?
2. Do you feel comfortable sharing your ideas with others?
3. Have you found tactics that are helpful in debating your ideas?
4. How do you react when you disagree with others about decisions that will affect your tasks at work?
5. Is it difficult for you to stand up for what you believe to be the best way to handle an issue? If so, why?

7

Is This Job Right for You?

A job, like a pair of pants, feels good when the fit is right.

Have you stopped to consider that you may be at odds with the people at work because you are in the wrong life cycle of your business? A company grows and goes through developmental changes just as humans do. As the company matures, each stage has predictable characteristics that require employees and leadership with different visions and abilities. You won't be happy if *who you are* is a misfit for the life cycle of the company—and you might blame the tension and clashes on your co-workers or leadership.

Lawrence M. Miller clearly delineates business life cycles in his book *Barbarians to Bureaucrats*.[1] The first stage of every new enterprise is like a newborn or young child: flexible, curious, moving in multiple directions, and changeable. This is the visionary and entrepreneurial stage that requires a charismatic leader of great vision who motivates others. Risk, excitement, and flexibility are inherent traits. As the business grows, just as a child maturing to young adulthood, maturity demands the establishment of systems, regulations, and less flexibility. A strong, single-minded, commanding, and decisive leader takes the reins.

A company culture has a personality as distinctive as a human personality.

In the early stage of a company's adulthood, employees are still energized by their contribution to the business's vision and growth. But as the administrative structure grows, the company ages. Focus shifts from serving a customer base and developing product quality to profit and benefits. In this stage bureaucratic leadership will exile innovators. If the company becomes part of inherited wealth, the aristocrat is often more interested in the income than the real work of the business. The employees feel stifled and become disinterested. The business experiences gradual decline, or even death, unless a new leader is found who energizes the employees and customers by balancing structure and administration with growth and vision, creating synergy.

Developmental Stages of Business	Developmental Stages of People
I. Visionary and Entrepreneurial	I. Child through Young Adult
• Flexible and changeable	
• Moving in multiple directions	
II. Stabilizing and Expanding	II. Middle Age
• Establishing administration	
• Developing systems	
III. Overseeing Established Systems and Administration	III. Mature Adult
• Powerful administrators grow rules and structure	
• Regulations demand conformity	
IV. Death or Synergy (Rebirth in Structure)	IV. Death
• Aristocrat inherits and plays at the business	
• Synergist balances vision, structure, and growth	

Visionary/Entrepreneurial Stage

Bruce Wilkinson is a prime example of a perfect fit for the visionary/ entrepreneurial stage of business. Bruce has birthed and grown multiple organizations into young adulthood: Walk Thru the Bible, Co-Mission, World Teach, and Dream for Africa. Each ministry has become an international program. His first ministry, Walk Thru the Bible, conducts more seminars throughout the world than any other outreach, religious or secular. It has created the largest faculty of Bible teachers ever assembled. Co-Mission sent thousands to teach ethics in Russian schools. In the first three years of its formation World Teach sent out six thousand teachers from forty nations to teach Bible studies. Dream for Africa ministers to students in African high schools.

Successful and fulfilled individuals find where who they are fits in the company's stage of development.

These ministries were Wilkinson's brainchildren. He birthed them, nurtured them, grew the ministry vision, energized his followers, stabilized its footing, then left each ministry in capable hands to start a new endeavor. How did he know it was time to leave? The ministry became work. Successful and fulfilled individuals find where *who they are* melds with the work they do.

If you work in a business whose culture is within the visionary/ entrepreneurial stage:

- Don't expect specific objectives or instructions, especially in the early development of the company. The mission is developing, growing, and flexing. This is the period of guidelines, not rules and regulations.
- Don't expect leadership to give you detailed follow-up of your work. The leader trusts you and will remain flexible to allow you to move as you recognize needs.

- If you are the leader, recognize you may have some people in the business who need more structure, so be willing to listen and allow these individuals to build some safety nets.

- If you work for the visionary, protect him from the people who want to box him in or crucify him for being too flexible and working for the long run, not this quarter's results.

- Recognize this may not be your stage if you are not energized and excited by risk and by moving out of secure zones, both requirements for the visionary/entrepreneurial stage of development.

- As this stage matures, the necessity for structure and more firmly set goals will become evident and crucial to its successful maturation.

Stabilizing/Expanding Stage

Steve Jobs was the ultimate example of the barbarian mentality that takes the ball and runs with it. He moved Apple from the envisioning stage to structure that set trends in innovation, products, and style for the world of information technology. He was the power broker, an idiosyncratic, individualistic entrepreneur, and is listed as either primary inventor or coinventor of over 230 awarded patents. His decisive leadership, quick decisions, oversight of minutiae, and iron-fisted rule were extremely successful in establishing Apple as the new flagship of technology gadgets. Yet some recoiled from his style of leadership, describing him as erratic, temperamental, an egomaniac, aggressive, and demanding. Jef Raskin, a former colleague, once said that Jobs "would have made an excellent king of France," alluding to Jobs's larger-than-life persona and command.[2] All complaints aside, this in-control giant was considered so important to the growth of Apple by those who know business

70

development that when Jobs announced his resignation from Apple in January 2011, Apple stock dropped.

If you work in a business whose culture is within the stabilizing/expanding stage:

- Be prepared for action. The goal is to refine, define, and stabilize as the company moves forward into a focused growth period. The direction of the business is settled and focused on carrying out its crystallized mission.
- Often this period is headed by a firm decision maker who isn't interested in long meetings or consensus decision making. She will make the decisions; you will carry them out. Quick decision is crucial to meeting the demands of fast growth, and rubs between the old ways and the new.
- This period is particularly exciting if you enjoy developing structure that focuses on the customer, product, or service. It requires high flexibility as changes in direction, personnel, and procedures will be made rapidly.
- At this stage people with sales or production skills will dominate the organization and neither have much use for "paper pushers" who develop systems.
- Encourage the "lion at the helm" to involve his team more, delegate more, and consider longer-range factors and outcomes. But don't be discouraged when decisions are made without such considerations.
- Employees will feel less flexibility as the organization matures and centers more on long-term goals than the "here and now."

Established Systems/Administration Stage

It is ironic that both companies and people seek comfort and security in rules and systems when those are the very conditions most likely to bring about decline. The mature company can find itself girdled by entitlements, structures, and regulations. The General Motors Company is a prime example of an established company with all the trappings of age and entitlement, as was evident when their executives arrived in their private jets to ask the US Congress for government loans—which, after they were given, became the impetus for a string of megabonuses and lavish vacations.

It is ironic that both companies and people seek comfort and security, when those are the very conditions that are most likely to bring about decline.

At this established-structure stage the company either slowly flounders into bankruptcy and eventual death, or someone is brought to the leadership helm who unites the employees and leadership, replanting a vision, restructuring, and making the necessary decisions outside of committee, formal structure, and administrative circles.

If you work in a business whose culture is within the established systems/administration stage:

- This is a period of specialization, a time when boundaries, systems, and structure have inflexible forms set by rules and regulations.
- Coordination between departments breaks down.
- The company culture focus moves from offense to defense: the shift from outward focus on the customer and quality of the product to inward focus on the bottom line and benefits, coinciding with the achievement of affluence.
- The process becomes more important than the product. Procedures, processes, systems of management, order, smooth operations, and consistency are priorities. More time is

72

devoted to checking up on financial reports and how things are done than focusing on why things are done and future growth of products, service, or customers.

- New products or services are expected to come from staff research or a development group, which can add to the alienation of those in the field selling the products and services. Creative ideas are overruled by planning committees. Employees are more likely to be rewarded for conformity than creativity.

- Flexibility and discipline are both lost as employees increasingly find ways to sneak around the formal system.

- Specialization leads to competence and efficiency, but motivation changes. Responsibility is now not for the whole, but for a narrow part; employees feel less connected and less valued.

- Those who inherit or lead the business may slip into conformity of what a "big business" should do, such as support cultural events, lead drives for charities, erect buildings that showcase success, acquire more companies and expand, or live up to Hollywood's version of a corporate executive lifestyle with airplanes, yachts, and so on.

Synergy Stage

Decline is not inevitable, only probable, when companies grow to be corporations, large partnerships, or conglomerates. The challenge is to find the mix of leadership that will spark vision and vitality that has become tangled in bureaucracy. The best-managed mature companies require a balance between the characteristics of visionaries, entrepreneurs, builders, and administrators. The company appreciates, rather than merely tolerates, diversity. It instills a sense of purpose, motivating the leadership, employees, customers, boards, stockholders, and even the general public.

Lee Iacocca was a synergist. He laid out a vision, offered hope, and enjoined the vision with the necessary structure to move the Chrysler Corporation from death throes to health. Iacocca began his engineering career at Ford Motor Company. After a short stint in the engineering department he moved to market-

Decline is not inevitable— only probable.

ing, where he quickly gained national recognition. He was involved with the design of several successful Ford automobiles, notably the Mustang, Lincoln Continental Mark III, Festiva, Pinto, and the revival of the Mercury brand. Eventually, he became the president of Ford Motor Company, but he clashed with Henry Ford II. After a thirty-two-year career with Ford Motor Company, including eight years as president, he was fired by Ford, despite the company posting a $2 billion profit for the year.

The Chrysler Corporation, then on the verge of bankruptcy, swiftly courted Iacocca. At the time the company was losing millions, largely due to recalls of the company's Dodge Aspen and Plymouth Volare, cars that Iacocca would later claim should never have been built. Iacocca turned Chrysler around. How? By downsizing; by winning approval of $1.5 billion in federal loan guarantees, which were repaid seven years earlier than required; by selling off unprofitable units such as the tank division and the European Chrysler division; by introducing timely products such as minivans, K-cars, and the Jeep Grand Cherokee; and by breaking the bonds of regulations and unnecessary systems that stymied and choked the company. In 1984 the company posted profits of $2.4 billion, one of business history's greatest comebacks. Iacocca energized a sense of pride in the corporation by his slogan: "If you can find a better car, buy it."

This may be where you fit if you find turning something around exciting, if you are unafraid to offer suggestions, and if you are willing to use your insights to help your company grow even if you know suggesting change has risk.

If you work in a business that requires synergy to resuscitate it:

- You must strive to find a decisive leader who is unafraid to change systems, break the bonds of bureaucracy, fire or change the role of employees, and reward creativity.
- It is the leader's ambition, her recognition and response to challenge, that determines whether growth is arrested at this stage.
- This can again be an exciting and hopeful period if you are a risk-taker and are willing to discard security for the possibility of great gain. If you work best within a structure or rules, you will find it difficult and chaotic to follow someone who seems be tearing apart the established structure.
- Trust in the leader as he decentralizes is fundamental to success in this stage, allowing everyone autonomy to manage his or her own area of the business.
- If you have a bureaucrat working for you, she will be better in a staff position than a line job where she will try to control and stifle creativity and demand order and conformity. In the staff, when she complains about others who are violating the sanctity of her systems, you can say, "So what?" This is difficult if key executives who wish to maintain control attempt to undermine change.

Finding Your Fit

I am sure you want your challenges at work to be with the tasks of the job, not the people with whom you work. Sometimes simply understanding that your company has a personality can free you from believing the tension should be credited to others in your job, and instead help you realize it belongs to the way things get done—the company culture. If you are a visionary, you will be uncomfortable and feel bound in the more mature stages of a company's development. If you prefer the boundaries and safety of regulations and set systems, you will find the flexibility and change in the early stages of a business disconcerting. If your chief concern for your job is to work within boundaries and limits, take your paycheck, and live your life after work, you will be happiest in the stage of specialization and regulation.

Don't be threatened if you find yourself struggling with changes in your company culture or in a new job. It may not be that you have changed. Sometimes as the company shifts, your skills and expectations no longer slip into the same grooves, even if you have been the perfect fit for dozens of years or were fine in your previous company. An engineer in a research and development (R&D) firm struggling to hire more engineers found that engineers who had worked in corporations that pigeonholed their abilities into highly specialized arenas struggled to meet the R&D requirement for a broader, more flexible perspective. He was forced to seek young engineers who could gear up to a malleable agenda. The more experienced engineers were far more skilled within their areas than the newly trained ones, but the speed and flexibility of the R&D company made it a misfit.

If you work for a company whose goals and business direction conflict with yours, if possible quit or ask for a transfer to a division in which you will feel more comfortable. You are better off working for someone whose goals and business culture value and reward your efforts. Be proactive. If you can't quit, perhaps you can retool for another position even as you continue your job.

The chief security guard, a twenty-seven-year employee, was assigned duties that doubled his workload when leadership changed. His request for a raise in salary was met with a notice that he could quit or change to another position. Wisely, the guard did not spin off about the maniacal personality of the new executive. He sought a different position where his experience could benefit both the company and satisfy his own needs.

Perhaps he recognized the CEO was reenergizing a sinking vessel. Or maybe he just recognized the futility of fighting against change. Either way, he was wise to seek a way to function within the system without feeling abused by overload. Likewise, be wise when the winds shift. Adjust your sails so that you can move through the shifting waters feeling your efforts are productive and rewarded.

How do you know the fit is not right? The same way Bruce Wilkerson did:

- Your job feels like work.
- You "itch" to do something different.
- You may feel comfortable with the goals but not the process being implemented to reach the objective.
- You feel the structure is too specialized, the regulations are too controlling, the bosses are off-base, the co-workers don't "get the picture."
- You wish the goals were less nebulous, or you wish they were more flexible.
- You dislike the constant changes or you dislike that nothing changes.
- You don't support your co-workers' or supervisor's actions.
- You feel boxed in, unable to use your talents.

- You feel a "nudge" that this job isn't right for you.
- You just don't like the way your work family thinks or acts.

Successful people don't have to be psychologists to think through whether *who they are* fits within the culture of their company. They figure it out just as the security guard did. You can too. I hope you appreciate that personalities and business stages, like the wind and a sail, are best fits when they work together. I also hope that if you are not in the right business culture or the business stage that fits your personality, you will have the courage to move on or retool to catch the figurative winds that will fill your sail and your soul with enthusiasm. Your job should be enjoyable, a place you feel you make a difference. It shouldn't feel like work.

Insights

- A company culture has a personality as distinctive as human personality.
- Successful and fulfilled individuals find where *who they are* melds with the work they do.
- Decline is not inevitable, only probable.
- It is ironic that both companies and people seek comfort and security, when those are the very conditions most likely to bring about decline.
- It is crucial for all who work together to appreciate, rather than merely tolerate, diversity.

Questions

1. What is it you like about your job?
2. What is it about your job that you do not like?

3. Do you feel you are on the same track as your co-workers?
4. Do you feel comfortable with the company's goals at this time?
5. If this stage of your company's development does not feel right, what might you do to move to another division, move to another company, or retool?

8

Bringing About Change

It is amazing what you can accomplish if you do not
care who gets the credit.

Harry S. Truman

Things are in pure chaos," he said. "I've been with the company
twenty years and knew what it would take to make it great. But
when I was appointed CEO everything I did to solve one problem
caused three more. What happened?"

Richard was genuinely puzzled. He seemed a super guy, so personality was going for him. And as we talked it was apparent his
knowledge was also not the problem. He knew the ins and outs of
every department. But therein lay the problem. *Knowledge* armed
him with goals, and superman that he was, he started out of the
gate full-speed ahead. He asked me, "You are suggesting I would
have been better off not knowing the problems?"

"No, of course not," I said. "Let me tell you a story of a friend's experience. He was in the Navy and had worked in the supply division for almost fifteen years. The naval ships were short on ordered supplies. Attempts to resolve the problem were met with excuses, jams in the warehouse, broken down transportation lines, and mishandled accounting. Intent on resolving the predicament, an admiral appointed my friend, a lieutenant, to head the supply command. He queried his new appointee, "What is the first thing you want to do?" Quickly the lieutenant responded, 'Sir, I plan to put my finger in the dyke!' The commander shook his head, and said, "No, son, you are to do *nothing*."

Thinking the commander did not realize how well he knew the issues that needed to be resolved, he argued, "But, sir, I understand the problems and what needs to change." The naval commander replied, "The issue is not *knowledge*; it is *trust*. You may have worked in the supply unit, but as head you are the new guy. You haven't earned trust as a leader. At best, those working with you are willing to give you a chance, but at worst they aren't sure you deserve the promotion. Take your time. You need a support group behind you or any attempts to bring about change will cause the dyke to fail."

There is a crucial "wait it out" period before those who will implement the process, those under your leadership at any level, will support a shift in power structure. That is true for any change in position, process, or behavior. (The one exception to this is when others see the situation as a crisis, a state of emergency.) This waiting period allows time for you to appreciate the intricacies of your new role, just as it allows your team time to buy into your modus operandi. Walk in, issue directives, move people around—and you may end up a casualty of the recoil, instead of the white knight correcting the ills of the workplace. That is what happened to Richard.

Richard did not recognize that even though as "one of the guys" he knew what changes were needed, his Johnny-on-the-run charge to bring them about would cause a pullback reaction. Employees are invested in the "old" ways. Change puts their babies under attack. Rush in and they go emotionally into an empty-nest syndrome. They may know their kid needs to grow up, leave for college, and become an adult, but it is hard to let go. Richard was yanking the old ways out of the nest, and suddenly even those who wanted change felt threatened.

> *The first and most important rule when change must take place: do nothing!*

Change threatens turf. Crucial to change is changing the *esprit de corps* from self-serving or territorial to team play. It's not that anyone says out loud, "This is my way, my project, my design," but if that's the way it was done before, you can be certain whoever oversaw that leg of the business was invested in it. It is personal, replete with their ideas, their suggestions, and their talent. The disjointed puzzle you are hired to put back together is manned by employees staking and protecting their claims. They may very well know change is needed. Let them partner with you to make it happen.

Change is about risk. Risk is part of business. But, like it or not, most employees establish boundaries and put up fences to protect against risk. So you won't be successful in making changes if you go at it like you are running a sprint. Real change is a marathon, a well-strategized plan, whether it is working with the crank beside you, the know-it-all above you, or the wimp under you. Successful implementation of change requires a slow process, almost like slow-cooking a roast. You can fire it up and cook it more quickly, but the meat will burn on the outside. Bake it slowly and the whole roast will be tender from the inside out.

Handling the Bear Challenges

Richard was stunned by the spin-back from some of the very people he considered friends. His attempts to quell their standoffishness and blatant negativity did nothing. He needed a "you've got to grow up, son" session. Every change will bring bears out of the woods to challenge your right to play in their forest. Be prepared. On the other hand, when things are askew at work the employees know it. They want the business to succeed and will be willing to help make it so—if first you slow down and give them time to begin saying, "I wonder if he is going to address this problem?"

Most employees establish boundaries and put up fences to protect their turf against risk.

Until that time has come, you will need to handle the challenges quietly. Everyone is watching. Richard needed to use the Rosalyn Carter tactic. On Phil Donahue's television program, he interviewed First Lady Rosalyn Carter. The interview began with a five-minute soliloquy by Donahue about President Jimmy Carter's terrible political decisions—the high inflation, the canceled Olympic games, the failed diplomacies. The live audience and those watching the debacle on television were stunned by his disrespect. No question that Donahue had legitimate points, but why was he trying to make mincemeat of the president's wife? The empathetic audience awaited Rosalyn's reply to his tirade. Donahue finally ended with the question, "Now what do you say to that?" She paused, smiled demurely, and remarked, "You know I don't really understand a thing you said, but I do know that Jimmy always tries to do what he believes is best for our country."

First Lady Carter refused to get into a dogfight. She denigrated the remarks by blithely moving on to the next subject, *refusing to give his negative appraisals the power of dialogue*. In every company there is a Madame Know-It-All or Mr. I've-Got-a-Better-Plan that threatens to keep everyone edgy—unless the leader simply refuses to acknowledge the individual as a threat. The success of a real leader is dependent upon his servant attitude. He joins hands with all, listening to "enemies" as well as supporters, but then, as Rosalyn did, moves on with his unspoken agenda.

All leaders will deal with those whose disapproval is outright, but sometimes the wolf in the den is one who whispers advice in the leader's ear. President Ronald Regan, when he was negotiating with the Russians to stop the stockpiling of nuclear weapons, was often quoted as saying, "Trust, but verify." Another way to say that is listen shrewdly. Even great leaders with much experience can be caught off-balance by advice that stabs. Remember Julius Caesar was not only taken aback, but removed from power, by the knife of his friend Brutus. Ultimately you are responsible for any course of action taken. Make sure you are aware of the long-term consequences of your strategy, regardless of how many people have affirmed it. As President Harry Truman said, "The buck stops here."

> *Refuse to get into a dogfight when you are challenged.*

Richard was also dealing with some tough *personalized hammers* that threatened to destroy the morale of a team. He knew each employee was responsible for disallowing hurtful behavior and for figuring out how to deal with those who were off-balance, out to lunch, or downright Machiavellian. But in almost every business an issue will surprise everyone with its potential to divide and thwart forward movement, an issue that demands leadership's involvement. The leader must take steps in such cases to allay potential damage to morale. Such issues have their own signatures, but they have in common their threat to unity.

Richard was aware that his minister had recently addressed a potentially divisive issue. The youth minister's wife had left him.

The minister called the young man into his office and said, "Go home! As of right now you are on a paid sabbatical. Figure out your life."

That seemed rather harsh, so I asked Richard to elaborate. Why did the pastor react against the "innocent" in the scenario? "He had no choice!" Richard replied. "The church would have divided—

*A*ppreciate each person's personalized hammer, his or her tactic for getting what they want.

some in support of the youth minister, some in support of his wife. Divorce might be the eventuality, but until the issue was resolved one way or another, emotions would be streaming and everyone would be affected." Richard's appraisal of the situation was astute. He then told me how he dealt with an engineer who had the reputation of being a Tom Sawyer. By numerous maneuvers, the engineer wormed his way out of much of his workload. "I called him in, advised him I was very aware of his work pattern, and gave him a choice: do your own work or quit." Richard was no pushover.

Still, as Richard admitted, in his new position he was off to a rough start. My advice to him was to restart. If he restarted the engine and it failed, at least he would have tried. If he continued down the same path, trying to address the issues on his own, the problems were going to volcano. "Call in the company heads and name it a new day. Have a slogan in hand. Do a Stanton!" I suggested.

Dr. Paul Eugene Stanton Jr. provides remarkable leadership to East Tennessee State, a small community university. The hundred-year-old school was barely on the radar when he became president. It was struggling through a rough patch with its former leadership and had slim community support. He immediately began an ETSU Pride campaign: "Get on the ETSU Express." He encouraged businesses and individuals in the surrounding communities to put out blue and gold signs welcoming students back, to attend sports and arts events, and to become involved. And they did!

Today, fifteen years later, ETSU is one of about two dozen universities in the country with fully accredited colleges of medicine, pharmacy, and public health. In fact, the only other university in the country that has the same range of health science programs (including audiology, speech pathology, radiography, nursing, public health, dental hygiene, and cardiopulmonary) is Ohio State University. The university houses strong master and doctoral programs in arts, sciences, and sports, as well as research development.

How did Dr. Stanton provide such dynamic leadership to catalyze radical change in such a short time? The answer: intentionally partnering a few goals at a time. In the annual ETSU Foundation meeting Dr. Stanton holds up his planned agenda for the coming year, the same kind he does every year. It's a five by seven sheet of paper with five handwritten goals. Each goal is farmed out, analyzed, spun around, and thought through by numerous people, who in the process join hands to support its development. It is this same type of sheet that suggested creating new doctoral programs and courageously exploring the termination of the football program to divert millions of dollars to strengthen the university's academic program and bolster other sports areas. Slowly, deliberately, building trust and momentum, the ETSU Express changed the university image. ETSU, as well as creating significant change within university programs, now boasts one of the strongest donor and alumni support bases in the country.

I encouraged Richard to not give up. Leadership is always challenging. I observed in him the same gifts as Dr. Stanton: insight, caring, and the personality to join hands. Importantly, neither Dr. Stanton nor Richard care about who gets the credit! They just want to help their business grow in healthy ways for the sake of all.

Let's look at the six main components that offer the best hope to bring about change:

1. Listen.
2. Analyze the situation needing change.
3. Take emotion out of it.
4. Think through goals.
5. Partner with others to consider whether goals are viable through the investigation and committee process.
6. Join hands so all feel change is a unified effort.

At that moment a squirrel jumped in a branch nearby. I asked Richard if he enjoyed watching the squirrels scamper among the many trees on his company's grounds. They seemed so intent on jumping distances that were far out of reach. Occasionally, a squirrel would jump an impossible length and miss his target. "Richard, I've seen hundreds of squirrels jump like that and have never seen any hurt trying," I said. "I guess they've got to take risks if they don't want to spend their whole lives in one tree. Maybe you have taken a few jumps to the wrong branch, but you can scamper back up. My guess is that if you say, 'Come on. We're in this together,' you'll turn things around."

Insights

- The first and most important rule when change takes place: do nothing!
- A well-strategized plan takes time and partners.
- Employees establish boundaries and put up fences to protect their territory against risk.

88

- Appreciate each person's personalized hammer, his or her tactic for getting what they want.
- Do not give negative actions the power of dialogue.
- Refuse to get into a dogfight when you are challenged.
- Appreciate that sometimes the wolf in the den is one who whispers advice in your ear.
- Trust, but verify.

Questions

1. Have you been successful in positions of leadership? What do you feel were some of your strengths?
2. Have you struggled in positions of leadership? Would other tactics have helped?
3. Sometimes the mix seems to be wrong between the leadership and those under them. In such cases, what do you recommend to help those caught in the crossfire?

9

The Generation Problem

Respect is like a boomerang: give it away and it always
comes back.

At 30,000 feet, somewhere between Park City and Atlanta,
the gentleman beside me asked me what I did. "At the moment," I replied, putting aside the notes I was scribbling, "I am
working on a manuscript about problems we encounter with our
co-workers."

He responded, "I could list some doozies for you! In fact, if
you are the expert maybe you could answer this: What has happened to this generation? Kids entering the job market today
are on their own wavelength. They check in late, leave early, and
even quit without notice if someone or something ticks them
off. They have no respect for anyone over thirty. This morning
I asked an intern a question face-to-face. He wanted to know
why I didn't just email. There are five steps between our desks.

Good gad! How can we turn our economy around with this new workforce?"

This man in the plane with me was discouraged by what he interpreted as the irresponsible and self-interested attitude of the "now generation." He was stymied by what he labeled as a blasé attitude. And he isn't alone in his puzzling. Many in business are in the throes of despair dealing with intergenerational, intercultural, and international employees. He was right; things are changing and, like it or not, he's part of the past.

Getting along in the work family has been critical in all ages for emotional peace, but not so much for business success. The standards, rules, and culturally accepted handshakes kept the business end of things in balance even if employees did not get along. Today, joining hands in the ever-widening gap between generations and accelerated pace of cultural change is no easy task. Today's employee walks out if relationships are askew or she feels stirred to try something new, costing the company thousands of dollars in training and lost productivity. How are we to handle misunderstandings between generations with equanimity? Is it possible to be as considerate of generational differences as we are of dissimilar customs in our international business partnerships?

Jessica Stollings Strang founded Re-Generations to bridge the gap in understanding between the four generations now engaged in the workforce. She leads seminars with businesses, ministries, nonprofit organizations, and even Congress, discussing the vastly divergent attitudes and work ethics of the generations. Jessica gets it! The generations speak different languages, as different as Chinese from English. Their view of work is poles apart. That is because each generation or culture has values programmed by their life observations and experiences.

Depression babies became part of the 1940s workforce in the midst of a war. The Greatest Generation was tutored in discipline, tradition, faith, loyalty, patriotism, and respect for authority, and wanted to leave a better world and legacies for their children. Employer and employee valued loyalty and stability. Work came first, family and friends next, and self last.

Misunderstanding and miscommunication aren't one-sided.

Their children, the Boomers, grew up energized by the optimism of President John F. Kennedy and space travel, and internalized complaints over Dad's constant work and Mom's slaving to can and clean. They disliked curfews, boundaries, and weekly treks to every church service. As young adults they entered the workforce in the 1960s intent on climbing the corporate ladder, changing social structures, and providing goodies and vacations for their family. They bounced around a bit more in their careers but, for the most part, remained with the company that promised to provide retirement benefits. Unfortunately, even as their degree of loyalty was different from that of the previous generation, the company's loyalty was also changed. Many companies used retirement funds for business growth and downsized the aged in preference to younger, less costly employees.

Boomers' children, those under age forty, are the Gen-Xers and Millennials, who grew up with both parents stressed by jobs that provided wealth but little quality family time. They were often latchkey children who dealt with divorce's grief and reality TV. They were overprotected, overdriven in academics and sports, overmedicated, and overrewarded by parents who felt they were giving what they had not gotten: pats on the back and lots of goodies. These younger generations value flexibility, quick rewards, positive feedback, technology, enough money to get by, and relationships—but not commitment. They are expected to have as many as fourteen different jobs and three different career tracks before retirement.

"Getting the four generations now in the workplace to successfully work together seems an insurmountable and daunting problem but, though it is tricky, it is crucial to success," declares Jessica in her seminars. "Imagine the simple issue of a year-end gift: a Traditionalist (the Greatest Generation) may favor a honey-glazed ham for the holidays. A Baby Boomer likely prefers a big, fat bonus check. What about a Gen-Xer or Millennial? Time off, of course, to ski with friends."

Jessica, who is part of the under-thirty workforce, reminisced about her own foray into the work world.

> I panicked my first day at work. I understood my job responsibilities but did not know whether I should treat my boss as my friend or as an untouchable. On the anniversary of my working in the company for one year, my friends surprised me with a celebration party. If I had been one of my boss's generation I would have marked the occasion as a milestone. Instead, I was shocked to see the banner—ONE YEAR! GO FOR IT GIRL! I felt like a deer in the headlights. Only old people settled into one job.[1]

Jessica's comment reminded me of a conversation I had with a civil servant who worked for President Jimmy Carter's White House social staff and now served in another public service arena. This was no bungling whiner, but she was lamenting about the generation problem. "I have worked for city government almost twenty-five years. Last year my promotion was passed over to bring in new 'energy.' The 'energy' is about to turn thirty, and believe me, he is wet behind the ears! It's tough to work for someone half my age—but even tougher when he labels me out-of-date!" I imagine there is another side to this story: the young executive who is equally frustrated when his ideas are met by "tried it and it didn't work" statements flowing from those who have been in the job longer.

Understanding the Change

In the past business was held together, even if employees did not get along, by cultural uniformity and established standards. Today the multiple generations struggle to understand each other amidst exponential change that produces a sense of instability, even to those who feel energized by change. Old jobs are axed, and new jobs are birthed and die in the blink of an eye. Technology is exponentially changing information channels and social structures. The world population and education programs are changing economic realities.

In the past business was held together, even if employees did not get along, by cultural uniformity and established standards.

Below I have highlighted just a few of the changes in our business and social culture as explained in a YouTube video created by Dr. Karl Fish and Dr. Scott McLeod. Their goal is to change our education system to meet the increasing demand for speed, flexibility, and multitasking. Staying abreast with changes is crucial to business success. Still, as you reflect on these shifts, is there any question why we are experiencing a widening gap and tension, internally and externally?[2]

1. Technology is changing the information channels that affect the way we learn, work, and live.

We are currently preparing kids for jobs that do not exist yet, for technologies that have not been invented, to solve problems we don't even know are problems.

- The top ten jobs in demand in 2010 did not exist in 2004.

- The US Department of Labor estimates that today's graduate will have ten to fourteen jobs by the age of thirty-eight; one in four workers has been with their current employer for less than one year; one in two workers has been with their current employer for less than five years.

- In 1984 there were no internet devices, in 1992 there were 250,000, and in 2008 there were 1 trillion.

- At the same time advertising, education, and news-dependent hard copy business is experiencing a death march, the dispersion of internet information has soared, making more information instantly available than was available in the previous five thousand years.

- A full 93 percent of Americans own a cell phone with a computer chip that is a million times cheaper, a thousand times more powerful, and a hundred thousand times smaller than one computer at MIT in 1965.

- Cell phone use is tripling every six months and is expected to do so for the next twenty years, with texting becoming the function of choice to those under twenty-five. The number of texts sent each day exceeds the world's population, with the average teen receiving 2,272 messages a year.

- Radio took thirty-eight years to reach an audience of fifty million; television thirteen years; internet four years; iPod three years; and Facebook two years.

- Technology is advancing so rapidly that a student starting a technical degree will by his junior year find that half of what he learned his first year is outdated.

2. Economic changes are driven by technology and world population shifts.

- Population growth is driving markets and available manpower. For every baby born in the United States, six are born in India, and more than four are born in China.

- In India, 25 percent of its 2012 population with the highest IQ is greater than the entire population of America. For every US college graduate, China and India have three graduates.

- China will soon be the largest country in the world speaking the language of business: English.

- By 2050, the Latin population of America will be its largest population sector.

- Women in America are now 52 percent of those in professional graduate programs.

- A full 50 percent of internet programs have been designed by those under the age of twenty-one.

3. Social changes are resulting in worldwide change.

- Media is sparking worldwide cultural uniformity.

- Religion is being seen as individual and separate from the business world.

- Serial monogamy is the wave of the future.

- One out of eight couples marrying in America today met on the internet.

- Women are now as engaged as men in the workplace outside the home, and though salaries are not yet equal, the gender gap is quickly closing.

- Conglomerates are eating small family-owned businesses.

- New realities, such as 70 percent of four-year-olds in America using a computer for games, are causing needed change in education focus and technique.

Wisely Working Together

I asked a young man how he liked his job at a coffee shop. He was elated to tell about his flexible hours and the company's willingness to let him off for pop-up opportunities such as snowboarding. He talked about his co-workers pouring themselves into caring for each other, like family. An older woman overheard the conversation, and remarked, "Just shows you how irresponsible these young people are, 'popping off' here and there, joking around instead of getting serious about their job responsibilities." You, too, may consider this young man's reply to highlight the immaturity and appalling work ethic of his generation. But what does he think about your shouldering the workload or overload at work? He thinks your priorities are out of balance.

The younger generations have the technology expertise; they want to learn business. Those with graying hair understand business; they want to learn technology.

So how do we join hands in our work family in the midst of exponential change with those who hold tightly to the old ways—or are so geared to the new that they chuck off all advice as passé? How, when these values are ingrained, do we appreciate each other? The answer is not simple, yet economic stability depends upon intergenerational and intercultural joining of hands.

The wise are riding the waves together. Mark Zuckerberg and Eduardo Saverin launched Facebook in 2004, their sophomore year at Harvard. Seven years later the company is valued at six billion dollars, but it took joining hands with business-knowledgeable old-timers to launch it to such heights. Joining forces is always difficult. Zuckerberg fought his partner Saverin against joining with the gray heads to reap financial gain from Facebook. What did *they* know about technology? Not much, compared to Zuckerberg. But they did know business.

If you are the older generation, older than forty:

- Become a mentor, a coach. The younger generation desires relationships.
- Ask questions, rather than detailing information, to encourage thought about the customer and business side of your company.
- Appreciate the gifts and consider thoughtfully the suggestions of the younger generation.
- Be open to new possibilities.
- As with a teenager, learn to pick your battles.
- Don't be intimidated by what you may consider brashness. For instance, if you want to be called "Mr." rather than "Joe," say so. If you require a dress code, say so—and explain the rationale behind the requirement.

If you are the younger generation, younger than forty:

- Recognize there is value to rules and boundaries.
- Be willing to ask "why" questions.
- Share ideas about change in a way that respects the past.
- Appreciate that many of your customers or co-workers do think differently, so value and respect those differences.
- Be excited about sharing your technology skills and understanding of its impact on your business with those who are intimidated and anxious about such radical change.

- Do not use labels such as "old hat," "outdated," and so forth.
- Remember that tact and respect are critical to networking.
- Though you may feel you are an equal, others may think you have not earned such respect. As they recognize your willingness to help them bridge gaps, you will become an integral, respected part of the team. Age will be irrelevant.

> *The fountain of youth is not a pill; it springs from challenges that energize the mind and spirit.*

Success in business no longer requires white hair. Nor does having years of business experience mean boredom. The fountain of youth is not a pill; it springs from challenges that energize the mind and spirit. And guaranteed: working with four generations in one workplace is challenging. This is the most exciting time of history—and, to think, you are part of it! That is, if you learn to get along.

Insights

- Misunderstanding and miscommunication aren't one-sided.
- In the past business was held together by cultural uniformity and established standards, even if employees did not get along.
- Today technology is exponentially changing information channels and social structures.
- The world population and education programs are changing economic realities.
- Survival and economic stability depend upon intergenerational and intercultural joining of hands.
- The fountain of youth is not a pill; it springs from challenges that energize the mind and spirit.

Questions

1. What changes are you experiencing in your workplace?
2. Do you feel good about the way the generations are working together?
3. What could you do that might build appreciation for the skills each generation brings to the table?

10

Minding the Family Store

Nothing tests one's mettle like working with family!

Did you know that family-owned businesses form the backbone of the American economy? Family businesses account for 50 percent of US gross domestic product and generate 60 percent of the country's employment, as well as 78 percent of all new job creation. Were you aware that 35 percent of Fortune 500 companies are family-controlled?[1] Is that encouraging? After all, you are working hard to build your company, sacrificing precious family and leisure time to assure its expansion in the marketplace. Your company's healthy advance shows you have the know-how to make a business thrive.

However, only one in three family businesses survive into the second generation. Are you confident that it is possible to structure your company so it will be that one in three, like Walmart, News Corp, and Ford Motor Company, which succeeded in bringing the kids into the company's culture and leaving a family legacy to the next generation? If so, I'm sure you have a well-thought-out strategy to guarantee its successful transition. If not, your business may be on the way to its demise; unfortunately, its passing away may bring down more than just your company. The legacy you hope to ensure your family security may, instead, be the death knell of your family.

Family businesses account for 50 percent of US gross domestic product, but only one in three survive into the second generation.

Generally speaking, the failure rate for all private businesses is high. According to the Small Business Administration's Office of Advocacy, 572,900 new businesses were launched in 2003 while 554,800 closed.[2] It's clear that businesses of any size have their own inherent risks and challenges to continuity, longevity, and ultimately success. But add the dynamics of family, and business may be like walking in a minefield, with explosions ready to blow apart the hard work of a generation. The question is, how do you continue the life and mission of your family business in a way that strengthens family bonds, rather than setting parent against child, brother against sister?

"You've got to get out of the box if you want to run a family business successfully," Lewis Wexler Sr. commented. This was advice from a man who carried into the third generation the successful tire company started by his father in 1919. Dan Wexler Sr. opened the doors of Free Service Tire Company to service automobiles. Cars were not very reliable in their infancy. Many a man found himself stranded, needing tires, air, water, or gasoline. The company's goal was to provide the best tire products to automobiles and service for stranded and ailing vehicles. Dan's son Lewis joined his father after college, growing and expanding the business, then successfully maneuvering through the problems incumbent in bringing his adult children into the growing business.

Today the century-old business is in its third generation of family leadership and has expanded to eleven retail stores, four wholesale centers for automobile and truck tires, and two retread plants in a four-state region. What makes this company different than so many other family-run companies that tried and failed? Lewis recognized the importance of leaving the identity (the box) of "child," or whatever family role, behind when as an adult that relative entered a business relationship in the workplace. Harrison, one of Lewis's sons, suggested, "Perhaps we were able to succeed because my father was wise enough to bring us in with a plan. The ones of us who wanted to work in the company found our niche in it; the ones who had other life goals serve on the board." Lewis Jr. added, "It's all about the business, not just us. Yet, it is about us. It is part of our lives and we want to give it our all, together. We are all connected."

The Wexlers are successful because their plan contributed to building on individual strengths, rather than creating rivalries. Their business story is unique in multiple ways:

- The company has been family-led throughout its history.
- The hundred-year-old company continues the business they know and understand, even as they reshape it to fit the needs of their changing customer base.
- Family leadership is determined by ability and interest, not because of "entitlement."
- Everyone in the family benefits by the success and support of each other.
- The family not only works together, it plays together.

Contrast that to the many businesses you know who have gone down in flames when family members battled over turf, chose "honorary" positions, and sucked the business dry of its operating capital.

The Crash-and-Burn Syndrome

This entire book deals with getting along with difficult people in your workplace, but I assure you, the problems in a family business require not only this knowledge but also a sheer determination to put family contention to bed. Families in business together split over issues too insignificant to be more than a speck on anyone else's radar. There is a breather when you leave the job if you work with strangers. But there's no getting away from business and fractured relationship problems if you work with a family member—and then go home with them, or even if you only join together for holiday get-togethers. If the wheels of your family's automobile are not running smoothly before you begin working together, you are in for a bumpy ride.

Family business success requires sheer determination to put family rivalries to bed.

Perhaps the business does not die when a family member is employed. Instead, a family relationship is the victim. Henry Ford, the brilliant entrepreneur of the 1900s whose assembly line production ensured quick delivery of automobiles, created a car empire, the Ford Motor Company. But Henry was unable to work amicably with his adult son, Edsel, in the business. Henry was a doting father who encouraged Edsel, his only child, to tinker with cars from the time he waddled in wearing diapers to carry tools for his Dad. He was elated with Edsel's love of cars and design, but as Edsel matured, his ideas and focus were not utilitarian like his father's. He was interested in hydraulic brakes, speedsters, and style, a source of tension with his dad.[3]

Henry appointed Edsel president of the Ford Motor Company at twenty-five years of age as a calculated maneuver to effectively devalue the company stock; thus, Henry could buy out the small minority stockholders and assume total control of the company. He didn't intend to let his son steer the ship. The stories are legend of the way Henry manipulated and humiliated Edsel, overturning his plans, ridiculing his decisions, criticizing his "high-flying lifestyle," even yelling at him to shut up in front of the board brass. Typical was the tantrum Henry threw when Edsel began construction of an office building to replace the crowded quarters of the accounting and sales departments. "Ridiculous!" Henry bellowed, as he ordered all the furniture in the old office building removed. "There won't be a problem with overcrowding now that all the stuff is gone!"[4]

Do siblings fare better than parents working with children? Of course not! The pecking order doesn't magically go away when children become adults. Unfortunately, if carried into their business world, these fractures infect and affect those working with them. Such is obvious in literature and in life. Characters in the Talmud, Bible, and Koran are examples of siblings causing chaos. For instance, Cain murdered his "business rival" brother Abel; their family enterprise ended. Jacob stole his brother Esau's "birthright" stock from his father Isaac; Jacob was forced out of the company fold. Today's CBN news highlighted two family battles typical of many others: the heirs of Ringling Brothers Circus, Kenneth and Karen Feld, are suing each other over a dispute that turned into a physical fight between the two; British rock group Oasis's singer Liam Gallagher and his estranged brother, famous for their debut album "Definitely Maybe," are headed to court with band mate

Noel, who left the band in 2009 saying he couldn't work a day longer with those brothers, contract or not.

In contrast, working with family also offers the opportunity for unparalleled relationship closeness. I have talked with those who enthusiastically share, "I know my brother . . . mother . . . sister . . . cousin . . . watches out for all of us." They talk with pride of a child or spouse's accomplishments. Still, even those with positive family dynamics acknowledge problems getting along are surprise bugaboos! Sad but true, for every father who says, "I love working with my son or daughter," for every husband who enjoys being with his wife 24/7, for every family member who claims no one is as great to work with as her uncle, cousin, or the like, there are two others who cry out, "Get me out of this!"

The best advice for people who idealize working with family: be careful. If you work well together now, share responsibilities, respect each other, appreciate your differences, easily forgive, and keep business problems separate from your relationship at home, you have a good chance of success. If not, be aware that when you work with family you are entering into a relationship offering little time away from people who will know your coming and going—round-the-clock.

The Rules of the Family Game

There are seven unspoken business rules that are critical to business success, especially when family works together. Even following these will not guarantee all will be smooth, but failing to follow them will guarantee problems.

Rule one: first and foremost, create a plan.

Having a plan is crucial when bringing family into a business or turning it over through succession. Leaving it to a family member, or members, to figure out how to make the company work after the fact often leads to wars over turf, battles over business direction, and fights over distribution of money. Traditionally, the more heirs, the more havoc.

Perhaps your "baby" is a motel chain and restaurant business. Under the duress of your doctor's pronouncement—retire or die—you turn over your business empire to your two very competitive children who want to be involved in the company. How do you do so in a manner that catalyzes success as opposed to rivalry? Consider these realities:

- We work best in a position that matches our talents and interests.
- We need the training/education necessary to be our best in the position.
- To maximize our talents we must understand the strengths, weaknesses, and goals of the business.
- We must understand the marketplace needs in our business arena.
- We must respect what each person, especially a family member, brings to the company table.
- We must feel our authority is respected, even as we are part of a team.
- We are tied through rewards, stock, dividends, and the like to the company divisions so that our natural inclination is to encourage and support those in the areas we do not manage.

With consideration of these points, you are ready to lay out a plan. One, you acknowledge each heir's interests, making one "ruler" of your hotel business and the other "ruler" of the restaurant business. Two, you tie them together with stock incentives. Three, you help each understand he or she has the final stamp on decisions for his or her company division; yet each benefits by encouraging and helping the other. Will your company continue to be successful? That depends upon a host of variables, but at least you have laid out a plan. Now the work of creating a business with its ebb and flow will involve creative team play, just as it did for you as you were first building the company. No one can guarantee another will have the wherewithal to carry through, sacrifice, and strategize in an ever-changing marketplace, but through planning you have set the footprint in place that grants your prodigy the possibility of success.

It's crucial to have a plan.

Yet would you believe that if a group of twenty-five different family business owners were asked the question, "How many of you have a plan for bringing your family into the business when you retire?" the number of hands raised would be about the same as those raised in a cancer support group of twenty-five people who were asked, "How many of you have a life insurance plan?" The answer: one! Mom and Pop are often so busy keeping the ship afloat that the thought of retirement is not rattling around in their heads. One businesswoman told her daughter, "You better hope I stay around. This is going to be one huge mess when I die."

If you are left with a mess, get help. Without a blueprint for keeping the company on track you may end up as part of the two out of three who lose the family business. Send out an SOS to the professionals when the problems are overwhelming. Sometimes the forest of problems is too thick for the family to successfully traverse. Seek advice from someone with the particular skillset needed by the family, such as conflict resolution, financial or legal counsel, leadership and management development, or strategic planning. A little light may be all that is needed to find the pathway to family peace and business success.

Rule two: choose the right person for leadership or responsibility, regardless of birth order, age, or gender.

A family company is a business, not a play toy. Creating honorary jobs because someone is "family" or spiking salaries, benefits, or compensation for the sake of family fairness will eventually kill the company if the position does not warrant it. Find the right fit. The right fit requires competency, character, and commitment to do the particular work. Slowly, we are witnessing an increasing trend in family business leadership in allowing the family member most interested in growing the company to assume its reins. As a result, the number of women or younger siblings leading family firms has increased 40 percent since 1996.[5]

It is interesting to note that women tend to focus more on succession planning. Female-owned businesses have a 40 percent lower rate of family member attrition, tend to be more fiscally conservative, and carry less debt than male-owned businesses. "In many cases," says William O'Hara, author of *Centuries of Success*, "daughters get along with their fathers better than sons do. There isn't that male competitiveness in those relationships." Moreover, O'Hara says that in researching his book, which examines family businesses around the world that have survived two hundred years or more, he found that "in cases where families allowed women to provide leadership, they often saved the family business."[6]

Penny Chenery is an example of O'Hara's point. She was part of the family that owned Meadow Farm, a thoroughbred racing operation and horse breeding business in Virginia founded by her father, Christopher Chenery. Although it had been profitable, the stable began losing money in the latter part of the 1960s, exacerbated by Christopher Chenery's five-year illness. Penny Chenery's siblings planned to sell the operation on his passing. However, she had other ideas. The housewife of eighteen years and mother to four children took over management of the 2,798-acre farm, hired trainers, and groomed the racehorse Secretariat for the races.

It's important to choose the right person for the position, regardless of gender, age, or birth order.

Secretariat won the rare Triple Crown (the Kentucky Derby, the Preakness Stakes, and the Belmont Stakes) and is by many considered the greatest racing horse of all time. The farm, including stables, breeding, and racing, became very profitable once again—for the benefit of the whole family, who were happy to allow Penny to grow the operation.

Rule three: talk it out.

Wise leaders pacify potential problems and emotional outbursts by talking through issues on an individual basis, prior to group discussions such as board meetings, so that each person has a chance to think through the problems rather than reacting emotionally to "surprises." Being family, the leadership should have a good feel for undercurrents and discord. Slights, put-downs, sarcasm, cutting humor, or any other negative or hurtful patterns established in childhood or other roles such as marriage must be disallowed.

The trust factor is crucial. Most families use communiqués and board meetings to keep the information lines flowing. Some use the meetings for consensus votes to direct leadership; others choose to allow the leadership to make decisions without their involvement. The better the communication, the more likely family will trust the leadership.

- Actively communicate with family leadership inside and outside the company so that each member appreciates and understands the direction the company is being steered.

- Disallow slights, put-downs, sarcasm, cutting humor, or any other negative and hurtful patterns established in childhood or other roles such as marriage.
- Discussion is crucial. Listening respectfully is essential.

Rule four: define the responsibilities clearly.

Simply said, if you don't know the rules, you won't be able to play the game. It is unfair to expect a family member to have the knowledge to run a business by osmosis. If you are expecting someone in the family to be on track and steer in the right direction, stoke his furnace with every bit of wisdom in your possession. Be his encourager. Think through the problems together until he feels confident and you are certain he is knowledgeable of the possibilities and pitfalls. This is the time for you to show you are wise, not that you are a step ahead of your trainee. It isn't just knowing how to run the show that is crucial to success. Appreciating the delicate intricacies of how to lead is equally important. That is more often learned by example than by rules.

Rule five: keep quiet until emotions cool.

The family business requires even more intentional effort to stay focused on being fair, just, and respectful. No question, there is a higher sensitivity level between family members. It's not that anyone is thin-skinned; rather, family knows how to push the buttons that trigger reactions. You are right that each of us is responsible for how we behave, so why shouldn't you strike back when someone keeps lighting your fire? Because, like it or not, though good judgment does not allow another to tread upon you as if you were a rug, it mantles you with the responsibility to be gracious.

Being civil won't kill you, even if you are dealing with a jerk who feels she is the only one capable of appreciating the scope of the business world. You don't have to be best friends, even with a relative, but when family joins for events, being nice and refusing to get into a tussle regardless of any jabs gives you the upper hand. *It is surprising how many times a "dog" simply gives up growling when no one pays him any attention.*

Though good judgment does not allow another to tread upon you as if you were a rug, it mantles you with the responsibility to be gracious.

On days there are adamant disagreements, get on your big boy or big girl pants and be the adult. Refuse to play games that end up in circular debate, angry words, or accusations. Use your innate understanding of the family dynamics to reason through the unreasonable—or back off until a voice of reason can be heard. The time to discuss issues stirring your passion, especially with family, is when the emotions are under control. Vince Lombardi said it well: "Once you agree upon the price you and your family must pay for success, it enables you to ignore the minor hurts, the opponent's pressure, and the temporary failures."[7]

Try these tactics, the same as you use with a nonfamily employee, to control your actions and reactions:

- Use humor, not sarcastic cuts.
- Acknowledge the suggestion, idea, or problem.
- Question politely by repeating: "Is this what you are saying?"
- State that the issue is no longer up for debate.
- Be willing to restate the course of action, again and again, without rancor or defensiveness.
- State up front that you will not talk when you are being addressed in anger.
- Leave, politely: "I'll be happy to talk with you about this when . . ."

- Be realistic: anticipate irregular behavior, rather than allowing it to be a surprise, if such is normal for this family member.

Rule six: business is business; home is home.

Especially with family, keep it that way. Problems must be ironed out through the proper channels at work, not carried home to be fodder for pressuring family members to take sides or make decisions to keep someone appeased. Families that work together must find ways to leave work problems at work so that their play is fun time together. It is hard to be happy at Thanksgiving dinner if your spouse has given you nothing but negatives about the interaction she has encountered with a family member in the office, especially when you feel duty-bound to support that individual.

Business is business; home is home.

Rule seven: use three important words frequently with family.

Quite often it is said that "please" is a magic word. And it is, especially with family. But there two other words equally as important: "sorry" and "thanks." How many skirmishes would have ended without escalating into war if someone had merely put pride aside? Being appreciated and respected is as treasured by family as anyone else with whom you work, maybe even more.

Somewhere over the Rainbow

Each succeeding generation has its own ideas about taking the company forward—or whether, indeed, it wants to join the family business at all. Successful transition has always been crucial to the continued success of family businesses, and the next ten years will see a major increase in the number of companies facing that hurdle as more Baby Boomers begin to retire. There may be a pot

The three most important words when working with family are please, sorry, and thanks.

of gold in the family business if the family can hang together. But sometimes the best decision for family cohesiveness is to sell and distribute, or hire others to run the company store. That is a crossroads decision, a turning point, and one as personal as whether to stay or leave a marriage. Neither decision, joining the family business or selling out, is without some pain.

I hope when you look back at the path you chose, you will be able to say:

- I did my best.
- I did what I felt was right.
- I learned from the successes and failures.
- I grew to appreciate that some of the family "quirkiness" actually contributed to the business.
- I learned to listen to others.
- I am more able to control "me."
- I made a positive difference.
- I gave it my all.
- I am grateful for who I am and the family I have.

Insights

- It's crucial to have a plan.
- It's important to choose the right person for the position, regardless of gender, age, or birth order.
- Family business success depends upon putting family rivalries to bed.
- If you don't know the rules, you won't be able to play the game.

- Business is business; home is home. Keep it that way.
- Opportunity knocks on the doors of relationship, especially when you work with family.
- The three most important words when working with family are *please*, *sorry*, and *thanks*.
- Neither decision, joining the family business or selling out, is without some pain.
- It is surprising how many times a "dog" simply gives up growling when no one pays him any attention.
- Though good judgment does not allow another to tread upon you as if you were a rug, it mantles you with the responsibility to be gracious.

Questions

1. Have you been successful in bringing your family members into your business? If so, what has contributed to that success?
2. If you have been unsuccessful in bringing your family members into your business, what were some of the problems and why do you think you were unable to overcome them?
3. Do you have a business succession plan? If so, describe it.
4. If you leave the business without a plan, what do you think will happen to it?
5. Have you been able to keep work at work and family time as family time with family members who work in the business?
6. How have you kept discord between family working in the business from spreading to "taking sides" among family members inside or outside the company doors?

11

Held Hostage by Manipulation

It's not having your buttons pushed that is the problem;
it's pulling your trigger.

Vincent Edward Jackson's family nicknamed him "the wild boar hog" (later shortened to Bo) because he was so often in trouble. But in one area in school he excelled: sports. Auburn University offered him a scholarship to play football, play baseball, and run track for the Tigers. In 1985 he won the Heisman Trophy. He was drafted to play for the Oakland Raiders football team and the Kansas City Royals baseball team. Bo was the first athlete to be named an all-star in two professional sports. Very few people know his amazing sports career was almost derailed by an emotion-driven trigger in seventh grade.

Bo left school every afternoon afraid, terrorized by a bully. One afternoon he was knocked unconscious by the bully who ridiculed and embarrassed him in front of his friends. He was raging when he aroused. No way was he going to be beaten ever again by a kid, regardless of his size. Bo fled home, found his mother's handgun, and came back intent on killing the teen. He found his tormenter, screamed, and raised the gun. As he pulled the trigger, he heard a voice whisper, *Bo, kill him and you'll spend your life in jail being beaten up by other thugs just like him. That's not the way to win.* He turned the gun and the bullet went into a tree.

Bo was fortunate on three levels. First, he didn't kill his tormen- tor. Second, he knew what the bully did was wrong. Third, he knew his fear allowed the bully to control him. Still, he didn't know what to do about his problem.

Manipulation is seldom as blatant as that of the bully who harassed Bo Jackson. It is usually subtle, or if more recognizable boomerangs between abuse and care: today someone blasts you with negatives; tomorrow that same person rewards you. It hides behind shields that say "this is for your own good." It masks itself with kind words, rewards, humor, and subtle suggestions of potential gain. Devious or transparent, manipulation can hold you hostage and it always pushes your buttons.

Manipulation can hold you hostage.

The problem for us, as for Bo Jackson, is figuring out what to do about manipulation. It's not like someone stands up and shouts, "Hey, I'm going to get you to do what I want through a little bit of twisting or a great deal of bullying." Unless we are extremely keen and aware of our power to stave off manipulative tactics, we do the same as Bo: we give the bully what he wants because we are naive, we like the job, we need the promotion, we try to please, we don't want to be fired, or we have a kind heart.

Add to that the fact that unless manipulation is blatant, it isn't easy to discern. Most manipulation slowly cooks its target, like the frog in the pot of water that slowly heats. The frog gets used to the rising temperature; by the time he senses the danger he is in, he is too cooked to get out. Likewise, too often we simply react in response to the maneuvers, even as our emotions are stacking, until we're "knocked out." Now, like Bo, it is easier for us to pull out the "gun" than to calmly figure out how to stop these calculated tactics. We reason that enough is enough.

"The guy that drove me crazy used a wheelchair," one man told me. "He claimed to have a job injury that put him in the chair. We felt bad for the creep. He got to be like flypaper and we were the ones stuck, bogged down by his needs, complaints, and criticism. Lucky for us he was caught dancing at a club—no chair! We were bamboozled by a rolling chair tactic."

Traits of the Easily Manipulated

Manipulators can't hold you hostage unless you partner with them. You must be part of the game. According to Martin Kantor in his book *The Psychopathology of Everyday Life*, the following are vulnerable:

Too trusting: often assume that everyone else is honest, commit themselves to people they hardly know without checking credentials, and rarely question so-called experts

Too altruistic: too honest, too fair, too empathetic

Too impressionable: easily seduced by charmers

Too naive: cannot believe there are dishonest people in the world, or if there were they would not be allowed to operate

Too masochistic: lack of self-respect, unconsciously let others take advantage of them

Too narcissistic: prone to fall for unmerited flattery

Too greedy: easily enticed to do wrong for personal gain

Too immature: impaired judgment, believes exaggerated advertising claims

Too materialistic: easy prey for schemes

Too dependent: need to be loved increases gullibility

Too lonely: may accept any offer of human contact

Too impulsive: too quick to make snap decisions

Too frugal: cannot say no to a bargain even if they know the reason why it is so cheap[1]

Controlling the Situation

Deep down inside you know when the game is out of balance. Feelings of agitation, anxiety, and uneasiness stir as innate sensors pick up on clues: body language, slight irregularities in words or actions. Something isn't right with the praise, superficial charm, crocodile tears, money, approval, attention, apologies, public recognition, silent treatment, threats, guilt, sulking, crying, intimidation, fear, doubt, lies, or whatever else is needed to draw you into a web.

I find it interesting that experiments with eight- to nine-month-old toddlers show even these very young children read underlying motivation. If an adult drops an object accidentally, a baby will crawl over to pick it up and give it back to the adult. However, if the adult intentionally throws the object to the floor, the child will disregard it. Unfortunately our reasoning side, the side trained to be "nice" and "go the second mile," wants to argue, *Surely you aren't reading her right*, or, *He wouldn't be taking you for a ride*.

There are no arbitrary methods by which another can have power over us or even stir our emotions—unless we allow it. It takes partners to develop a screwed-up relationship. Manipulation rarely puts you in the well until it has let you dig the hole bit by bit.

1. Trust your instincts. If emotions feel iffy and are signaling a problem, pay attention!
2. Stay cool. You lose if you fail to keep your emotions in check. Allowing the manipulator to get under your skin is your choice.
3. Know you can't be forced to do what you choose not to do.
4. You are responsible for what you do and for what you allow.
5. Distinguish between someone who always wants a *handout* versus someone who wants a *hand up*.
6. Arm your arsenal of calm responses. State simply, "That's not how I see it," "That's not what I feel," "Sorry you feel that way," or "I'm sorry, but I will not do that because . . ." Use a bit of caring: "You must be having a bad day," or "I'm sorry you seem to be so down today." Address the presentation: "Sure, I can take a joke, but that wasn't a joke. It was a put-down," "That wasn't humorous, it was cruel," "You don't need to yell to be heard," or "I respond better to being asked than being commanded."
7. Do not condone manipulation by rewarding it. Consider the reward for those who are negative or don the pity-me robe: others don't ask them to do their fair workload share. Manipulators are masters at getting what they want.
8. Remember it is the responsibility of each of us to behave in ways that join, rather than divide.

In any pressure-loaded situation you must decide your course and talk through the issue as an adult. Most problems do not resolve themselves. They only get worse as time goes by and you, by your silence, comply. If you intend to change the pressure and its power in your life, you must talk about your options and state your limits and boundaries to the person who has the ability to bring about change. Do it honestly, quietly, and without rage, threats, or blame. Refuse to self-talk the negatives: *he won't listen; I've tried and it doesn't work; nothing ever changes.*

Inaction says you are willing to accept the status quo. Mature adults find ways to free themselves from emotions that spin around manipulative behavior, even if they are dealing with people who are playing their way and don't intend to change.

Give yourself the gift of time.

Seek counsel if the stress is getting to you. Sometimes a third party outside of the situation can help you see your way out of the forest. At the very least, he or she can let you vent and offer objective guidance. The best counsel is outside any office channels that could become a vehicle for gossip. If you are uncomfortable seeking *live* help, books and the internet tackle almost every topic imaginable. Deep inside, most of us know what we need to do but the consequences seem so daunting that we get locked. Let someone unlock your thoughts, not by telling you what to do, but rather by shining a light on the possibilities to alleviate part of your stress.

A young man shared his experience. "The hundredth ridiculous demand by my supervisor got to me," he said. "I refused to increase my workload any more. My manager said, 'Do it or else.' So I shrugged and said, 'Well, you can fire me right now, move me into another position, or I will give you my two weeks' notice.' He looked stunned, and said, 'Wow. I didn't expect that!' It was awesome to realize I did have some power in the game."

The employee was young, but he was mature enough to state his limits. Unfortunately, standing up for what was right also put his job in jeopardy. Sometimes our responsibilities, financial and home, make addressing manipulative behavior seem too costly.

But the more willing we are to discuss our feelings openly, calmly, and without rancor, the less likely we will find ourselves feeling at the mercy of someone's dictates, even if we choose to stay the course.

If you have difficulty saying no, please give yourself the gift of time. Say, "Thank you, I'll think about it. Let me get back to you." Time allows you to thoughtfully consider the tactful way to refuse or, if accepting, to set boundaries. Time gives you moments of reflection. It keeps you from stumbling in emotion.

Feeling sorrow instead of hurt turns angry fists into compassionate hands.

If you are stuck in a situation with someone whose maneuvering sets you on fire, it helps to affirm to yourself that the behavior is wrong. But it is equally important to do as Scripture says: "Bless your enemies." Talk nicely about the person who drives you crazy. Pity the person who drives others away by backdoor maneuvers. How sad to be so insecure, so cocksure, so caught in compulsive behaviors, or so unwilling to change destructive patterns that he or she stands alone as an island, rather than joining in an alliance. Feeling sorrow instead of hurt turns angry fists into compassionate hands. It keeps emotions from circling the negatives.

Almost everyone understands the term "business savvy." That means you have an astute understanding of things going on around you. You understand the ins and outs of the daily grind. You know what has come to pass and have a fairly good handle on what is in the pipeline for the future. You know when to speak up and when to be quiet. You are shrewd.

The term "shrewd" originated in the thirteenth century to describe someone who was a scoundrel. Through the ages the meaning has changed to imply that a shrewd businessman is both intelligent

No one controls you—unless you allow them control.

and practical. He guards and protects, considering his time at work as an investment. Shrewd people recognize that their skills, talents, and ethics make them a valuable asset to the business. They neither stomp nor pout about the problems, but neither do they allow anyone to pull the wool over their eyes. Be shrewd enough to be business savvy!

Insights

- Buttons are the danger signals that warn us of unresolved problems.
- It takes partners to develop a screwed-up relationship.
- No one controls you—unless you allow them control.
- Give yourself the gift of time.
- Feeling sorrow instead of hurt turns angry fists into compassionate hands.

Questions

1. Do you work with someone who uses manipulation to get his or her way?
2. What indicates to you that someone is manipulative?
3. Do you try to manipulate others, or do you seek to negotiate and compromise?
4. Do you address manipulation up front?
5. If so, share the experience and if you were you able to resolve the problem.

12

Changing Your Paradigm

I am what I think I am, not what others say I am.

As a professor of entrepreneurship I have the opportunity to interact with students from around the world, especially in the summer MBA classes I teach in the prestigious German Hochschule," explained Dr. Andrew Clark. "The classes are comprised of students from around the world. My goal is to break through the prejudices and glass ceilings that each brings with them from their culture, so that they might be successful in international business endeavors. To do so I expect their teams to create a business plan. I appoint the CEO and members of each team to specific company positions to cover marketing, management, finance, research, and development.

"I chose Amany, a young Muslim woman, to be CEO of a team because of her leadership potential, but she asked to be removed because as a Muslim woman she could not manage men. I replied,

'Amany, women are CEOs of businesses all over the world. You are taking this course for credit, and to pass you must serve in this role.' In turn, some of the men asked that Amany be removed because of the impropriety. I responded, 'Welcome to the world, men. Women are CEOs all over the world. Get over it if you want to get your MBA!'

"By the end of the course Amany had turned a rebellious group into a cohesive team. She thanked me for allowing her the opportunity to recognize the special gifts she offered to a team, regardless of its gender makeup. The men expressed surprise and a new appreciation of the skills and insights a woman brought to team cohesion and plan development."

> *We may be our own worst enemies if we see ceilings instead of opportunities.*

Amany is fortunate that at a young age the stereotype ingrained in her by culture was exposed and contradicted. How astounding and sad that even among the brightest and most educated worldwide, we continue to allow ourselves to be bound by arbitrary limits that stymie our potential. On the other hand, how encouraging it is to recognize *we can change.*

Dr. Clark now serves as professor of entrepreneurship at East Tennessee State University and teaches how to break through ceilings by utilizing individual skills and talents. He was jobless for more than a year after his division in a worldwide power brokering company was eliminated. He was too educated for many jobs, and too high up the management chain for others. Unfairness is not restricted by age, gender, education, or wealth. It was difficult for Dr. Clark to see the positive when house payments were due and doors were closed. "In the midst of that time it was tough to focus on what I might bring to the table, just as it was for Amany. I just wanted someone to offer me a seat!"

Changing the Negative to Positive

Recognizing that we do have a choice is the key difference between those who are stymied by glass ceilings and those who simply disregard superficial limitations to become successful. Amany's desire to pass Dr. Clark's course was more powerful than her obedience to the cultural dogma that said she was not as capable as a man. Others are hardwired with confidence that says, "I am capable."

Lois Bowie was born saying, "Why not?" She refused to see herself through the eyes of others. With three young children and a husband in graduate school in Iowa, she sought employment as a realtor in the largest firm in Davenport. Realty was a 100 percent male-dominated career in the mid-1900s. Though the president of the company laughed in her face, Lois clinched the job with the challenge that within one year she would be the firm's number one salesperson. She was—and continued to be so for the four years she lived in Iowa. In her career heyday she owned businesses in five states, employed thousands, and walked as coequal to anyone and everyone. She saw no ceilings and she was at war with no one; she was simply confident of her abilities. She didn't play by the cultural rules that implied her gender made her less able. She set her own ceiling by what she believed—or, in her case, did not believe.

It may not be a lack of confidence or cultural dogma that stymies your potential. Sometimes the voices of your upbringing keep you bound. Sarah Wells grew up in poverty. In eighth grade she dropped out of school to marry, and by age twenty-three had four children. Her husband left the family homeless when she was twenty-five. To survive, she took the jobs an uneducated mother could find. Today she has a graduate degree; is executive director of a Good Samaritan program that feeds, clothes, and shelters over 177,000 people yearly; has raised over thirty million dollars in funds and services; spoke before Congress about the needs of the indigent;

and is minister of a United Methodist church whose enrollment has doubled in four years. How? Desperation bred determination. Sarah quit listening to negative voices.

Charlie Oliver's father was a truck farmer, a good man, the salt of the earth, but never had more than a nickel in his pocket. His only sister was mentally challenged. Charlie was a little guy, never taller than 5'6". He was extremely bright, but there was no way for his family to help with the cost of an Ivy League college so he worked his way through a small state university in his hometown, majoring in the new field of computer science. His first job after college was with one of the world's leading chemical companies, where he helped establish the company's new computer programs in the early 1970s. Often his supervisors were given credit for Charlie's accomplishments. "It isn't fair!" bemoaned his wife, but Charlie reassured her that his goal wasn't personal recognition. He remembered his father's labor and was glad for a challenging job that was on the forefront of change!

Real change is most often born from the hot coals that make the current situation intolerable.

Charlie was eventually promoted to Rochester, NY, where he became head of Eastman Kodak's Worldwide Computing and Telecommunications. Thirty years later, he retired after traveling and establishing communications worldwide for Eastman Kodak. He had plenty of issues to raise the flags of prejudice: he was small in stature, from humble roots, attended an ordinary state university—and yet, in the world of big dogs, he kept rising to the top because he didn't have his fists up. He wasn't concerned with who got the credit or how someone might box him in an initial meeting. He focused on using his gifts and doing his best. His grace and perseverance broke down doors.

What did Dr. Clark and these three other people have in common? They didn't give up, nor did they bend to what others thought. History is full of stories of those who rose, even from ashes as Sarah did, to riches in character, empathy, insight—even wealth. Real change is most often born from the hot coals that make the current situation intolerable. Crisis and pain are its catalysts. There is a gut-wrenching moment when you cry out, "This is no longer acceptable." And you mean it! You will not go on as you are. Sarah Wells hit that point after nine times being forced onto the streets, homeless with four small children. She went to a minister and said, "Teach me!" She did not want a handout; she wanted a hand up.

Statistics repeatedly show that IQ, gender, education level, or any other determinant is not the crucial factor in success. It is one's belief that he or she can succeed that gives the self-confidence to keep on keeping on when others say it can't be done. It is your tenacity that finally puts you across the finish line.

These people had the same choice you and I have: look up or look down. It is so much easier to look down and wallow. It is nice in many ways to be a victim. People feel sorry for you. You have an excuse to do nothing: "I don't have . . . I'm not . . . I'm unworthy . . . incapable . . . useless . . . from bad stock." Winners say, "So what?" and then turn off the thoughts that shout, "You can't!" When my seven-year-old daughter died, I did not have to do another thing for the rest of my life. Do you know what others would have said? "Poor Betty. She's never been the same since her daughter's death!" How sad! This is the only life I have. To be locked on to a tragedy, a failure, or anything that prevents living to the fullest is the ultimate tragedy.

Paradigm change requires you to think:

- I do have a choice.
- I am not limited.

- I want a hand up, not a handout.
- I believe I can.

The Untold Secret

Here's what you will rarely hear: it's not just about you! If you want others to believe in you, believe in them. Believe they will give you a chance. Believe they are decent, caring individuals. Believe they want to help. There is a powerful adage: if you want a friend, ask for help. When someone helps you, they have a stake in your game. They want you to succeed. Dr. Clark wanted Amany to break through the barriers. He became her mentor. When she was discouraged, he cheered her forward. Her success became his success.

Seek a mentor, someone who believes in you, someone you respect, someone willing to teach you. Sarah Wells moved from a cycle of chaos to a productive, centered life because she was willing to seek help. Lois Bowie was given a chance because she challenged the company head. Charlie Oliver just kept doing his best as those around him benefited. Dr. Clark knocked on doors until someone actually told him, "Andy, I dreamed about you last night. I think you might be the very one to join our faculty at the university."

If you want others to believe in you, believe in them.

Each believed in his or her own ability. Perhaps you feel inferior because of race or gender or a non-Harvard education. Charlie Oliver and Sarah Wells will tell you that nothing stops your train unless you put on the brakes. Maybe you feel too young or that others will reject you. Amany recognized that as just a mind-set. Maybe you think you are too old or too educated. Dr. Clark would disagree.

Take Off Your Boxing Gloves

If you want the door to open, take off your boxing gloves. It may be true that people should accept you as you are, but if you want the job or to move up the ladder, get over it. Companies have requirements that have all to do with image. If you want to be part of the company, you must be willing to play the part. Be realistic about extraneous requirements. How?

- Dress the part.
- Look the people with whom you interact in the eye.
- Shake hands firmly.
- Be confident that your experience (as a woman, as physically handicapped, as over- or underqualified, or whatever seems to be your ceiling) has given you insight that will be valuable to the company.

Equally important, focusing on the positive in others frees you to believe in limitless possibilities for yourself. They are not perfect any more than you are. A little understanding goes a long way in whether people consider you a good choice for promotion and opportunity.

An employee told me he was considering leaving a job he loved because his boss was such a control freak. He was left in charge of the company store while the manager attended a seminar. Fifteen times during the week, the boss called to check on things. The employee felt distrusted, belittled, and angry. I suggested that the young man consider that his boss was a door-checker, the person who gets out of bed to recheck the doors after his wife says, "Yes, honey, I locked the doors." The wife has the opportunity to get angry and think, *Doesn't he trust me?* Or she has the opportunity to see her husband as her backup. The checking says more about the husband's compulsive need to oversee than her ability.

133

> *The more you refuse to define yourself by the actions or reactions of others, the more possibilities you will see for yourself.*

What if instead of considering the boss's behavior a threat, the employee laughed and thought himself fortunate to have a "backup" to provide some oversight that might occasionally catch slip-through-the-crack problems? Maybe the boss was checking in because he wanted affirmation that all was well with his "baby." Maybe the company was his identity, and he called to feel needed. There could be many reasons—none of which had to do with the employee's ability. The more you refuse to define yourself based on the actions or reactions of others, the more possibilities you will see for yourself.

Your Choice

Each of us should ask: Am I derailing my own opportunities by listening to negative voices that focus on what I can't do or what others will think of me? Each of us must figure out how to overcome the boundaries that are superimposed on us through reward, punishment, peer pressure, or cultural expectations. We may be our own worst enemies if we see limits instead of opportunities. It is sad to self-impose limits on our abilities because of the negative thoughts of others! Success in the business world depends upon which voices you allow to control your confidence. A world of possibilities is yours, or not—your choice.

Insights

- We may be our own worst enemies if we see ceilings instead of opportunities.

- Real change in our goals and view of our possibilities is often born from the hot coals that make our current situation intolerable.
- Ask for a hand up, not a handout.
- Thoughts do not have to be given the power of words.
- If you want others to believe in you, believe in them.
- The more you refuse to define yourself by the actions or reactions of others, the more possibilities you will see for yourself.

Success in the business world depends upon which voices you allow to control your confidence.

- I set my own ceiling by what I believe I can or cannot do.
- Success in the business world depends upon which voices you allow to control your confidence.

Questions

1. What paradigms need to change in the way you see yourself?
2. Are you finding that the way you see yourself harms or helps your relationships at work?
3. What could you do to change your paradigm?

13

Building Stress Absorbers into Your Life

A sense of community is to people what shock absorbers are to automobiles.

Our two Great Danes were diagnosed as having no immunity to mange, which is caused by a mite that burrows under an animal's skin. The skin exudes a serum to surround the mite. This irritation causes the animal to scratch the infected area, spreading the infection rapidly, and if untreated, the animal may die of exhaustion, dehydration, or secondary infection. The veterinarian assured us our dogs' mange could be cured—temporarily. The long-term prognosis was the stumper. Mange would return when the dogs were under stress. Did *stress* include such things as another dog entering our dogs' space or a car coming down our drive? It did! The dogs had no coping skills. Stress of any kind triggered their body chemistry, lowering their immunity to the burrowing mites.

Chronic stress in humans is like mange. It eats away at you. Prolonged or excessive stress, the kind that overwhelms your ability to cope, can take a severe psychological and physical toll. At first it may present as nagging irritation, edginess, chronic headaches, or increased susceptibility to colds. But, if there is no downtime, chronic stress levels can lead to depression, cardiovascular disease, musculoskeletal problems, impaired immune response and cancer, fertility problems, and a host of blood and digestive disorders. Emotions spin, causing outbursts, slowed thinking and responses, and fatigue. Stress also triggers an increased white blood cell count and activated macrophages, changes in liver metabolism, reduced sexual activity, and release of hormones such as cortisol and prolactin that initiate a cascade of events leading to swelling and pain.[1]

Your career, attitude, and health depend upon successfully managing stress.

During periods of high stress, such as tax season for accountants or exam time for medical students, significant increases in cholesterol levels are found even when there is little change in diet. In fact, a landmark twenty-year study conducted by the University of London concluded that unmanaged reactions to stress were a more dangerous risk factor for cancer and heart disease than either cigarette smoking or high cholesterol foods.[2] Dr. J. J. Lynch, author of many books on the health consequences of stress, states that following chronic emotional pressure or significant loss, a man's heart attack rate increases six times, strokes twelve times, suicide four times, accidents ten times, murder eight times, and cirrhosis of the liver and pneumonia seven times.[3]

Perhaps thinking of stress as rain is a good way to appreciate the effects of persistent stress. A little rain periodically is good. Even a great amount for a short time can be tolerated. It revs up energy, pumps chemicals to your brain, and floods the body with adrenaline to keep you alert. It can energize and motivate you to deal with challenges. But in the same way as continuous rain causes flooding, an overactivated autonomic nervous system eventually causes a breakdown in your health.

Job stress is costly, with an annual price tag for US businesses of over $300 billion due to increased absenteeism; employee turnover; diminished productivity; medical, legal, and insurance expenses; and workers' compensation payments. Put into perspective, that's ten times the cost of all strikes combined. Chronic pain, hypertension, and headaches—all stress-related ailments—account for 54 percent of all job absences as well as 75 to 90 percent of employee visits to hospitals for ailments linked to stress.[4]

Interestingly, job stress is more strongly associated with health complaints than financial or family problems. The NIOSH report from the CDC, Centers of Disease Control, is an excellent resource that cites the following:

- 40 percent of workers reported their job was very or extremely stressful.
- 25 percent view their jobs as the number-one stressor in their lives.
- 75 percent of employees believe that workers have more on-the-job stress than a generation ago.[5]

Tackling the Problem

"An estimated 1 million workers are absent every day due to stress. It is clear that men and women with demanding jobs that give them little control have three times the hypertension, as well as significantly more cancer and heart disease, as co-workers who feel they have control," writes Dr. J. J. Lynch.[6] So how do you lessen your workplace stress if you feel you have little control of the expectations of your job or the people with whom you work?

Stress is a mind game, and is directly proportional to how much you wrap your emotions around the problems in the job—the degree to which you care. That is why what stresses one person is merely a nuisance to another. If you didn't care, you would blow off the petty nuisances, the overwork demands, and rude behavior. Not caring, you could stand back, assess the problem, ascertain the possibilities, and devise a plan to distance yourself. You would do your best, shake off the irritations, and get the paycheck without caring what others did or thought of you. The problem is most of us do care.

> **Stress is directly proportional to how much you care.**

Many companies are starting to provide some type of stress management training to their employees as they recognize the increasing problem and cost of absenteeism and violence. The goal of the programs is to teach time management and relaxation skills, and to be an outlet for voiced frustration. While such programs are beneficial at least in the short term, they don't address the root causes of stress, which involve the dynamics of a work family and the balance between work and home demands.

You enable stress by feeling unable. Determining how you will handle your work issues empowers you and lessens the power of stress to damage your health and relationships. It keeps you focused. You may not be able to bring about the desired changes in your work or in the person who irritates you, but determining how to cope without being in a spin over the issues will keep stress from slowly eating away at your health! In times of great stress or adversity, it's best to keep busy, to plow your anger and energy into something positive as you tackle your problem.

For instance, if your professional commitment requires long work hours or travel that conflicts with duties at home, find a caregiver who will be available round-the-clock to handle your home needs (or an understanding partner) or explore the possibilities of change within your company. Neither of these options are a totally comfortable solution. Still, devising some sort of plan gives a degree of comfort from the knowledge that you have some control to alleviate part of the chaos.

These five keys outline the route from confusion to strategy:

1. Recognize what causes the tension.
2. Ascertain your options.
3. Consider the cost.
4. Know your limits.
5. Own your choice.

Build a Roseto Effect into Your Life

The most significant possibility for your lessening the negative factors of stress, however, has little to do with letting off steam in therapy, distancing yourself from your problems, or even determining a plan to deal with tension. It is what has become known as the Roseto Effect.

Roseto is a small community near Bangor, Pennsylvania. In January of 1882, a group of ten men and one boy left the small village of Roseto, Italy, where they worked in marble quarries in the surrounding hills or farmed the fields of the valleys below. They came to America in hopes of finding a better life for their families. The following year fifteen more *paesani* from Italy joined the group, sending word back to their families and neighbors about the promise of better jobs and an easier life.

You enable stress by feeling unable.

In Roseto, PA, they built homes where three generations lived together: grandparents, parents, and children. To be self-sufficient they terraced the hills to grow gardens and raise pigs, chickens, and cows. They built a church and invited a young priest to become their spiritual guide. He encouraged fraternal clubs and organized festivals. The town became a community of Italians who considered themselves family and lifelong friends, isolating themselves from the surrounding communities of Welsh, Germans, and English. Tight-knit Roseto seemed a diorama of what once was the nation's ideal lifestyle: neighbors who looked after one another, embodying the grassroots of American-style democracy, faith, and traditions. The village was a living laboratory of the effects of good neighborliness.[7]

Roseto was an anomaly that drew the attention of two doctors of research in the 1960s: Dr. Stewart Wolf, who taught in the medical school at the University of Oklahoma, and sociologist John Bruhn. In defiance of medical logic, the citizens of Roseto seemed nearly immune to one of the most common causes of death: heart attacks. Unexplainably, for men over sixty-five, the death rate from heart disease in Roseto was roughly half that of the United States as a whole, yet these men smoked and drank voluminously, worked in backbreaking, hazardous jobs, and ate an atrocious, heart-attack-in-the-making diet.[8]

In fact, the death rate from all causes in Roseto was 35 percent lower than the national average. There was no suicide, no alcoholism, and no drug addiction. No one was on welfare. They had no peptic ulcers. Villagers were dying simply of old age. Two other statistics in Roseto were eye-catching: both the crime rate and the applications for public assistance were zero. In addition, in a community where most of the first generation was illiterate, their children attended college at a rate far above the national average.[9]

Why? Certainly their lives were not easy. The men spent their days mining in nearby slate quarries. The women spent long hours in sewing factories. Their diet was a dietitian's nightmare—traditional Italian food floating in butter, cream, and cheese. They did no exercise, no yoga or Pilates. Researchers thought perhaps it was merely good genes, so they studied families in Roseto, Italy, and those who immigrated to other parts of the United States. These cousins did not share the same remarkable good health.[10] Then researchers investigated nearby Pennsylvania communities, thinking that perhaps the community's good health was the result of factors in the environment, but this was another dead end. For men over sixty-five in the nearby communities of Nazareth and Bangor, the death rate from heart disease was three times that of Roseto.

In their 1966 study entitled "The Power of the Clan," Wolf and Bruhn found several factors to be the discerning difference between the citizens of Roseto and those whose stressful lives led to multiple health problems, even with good diet and exercise:

- A joyous, supportive team spirit
- People encouraging people
- Spiritual sense of fulfilling a life purpose
- A clearly defined role in which one feels useful
- Conformity that reduces the stress of "keeping up" with others
- Working with a common goal
- Life swinging around traditions
- A sense of fulfilling commitments and handling responsibilities

It is clear that characteristics of a tight-knit community are better predictors of healthy hearts than are low levels of cholesterol or restraint from tobacco use. Isolated individuals tend to feel more overwhelmed by the problems of everyday life. Such a person internalizes stress, which, in turn, can adversely affect everything from blood pressure to kidney function. This is much less likely to be the outcome when a person is surrounded by caring friends, neighbors, and relatives who keep him or her grounded by traditions and faith. The sense of being supported reduces stress and the diseases it engenders. The study concluded that mutual respect and cooperation contribute to the health and welfare of a community and its inhabitants; self-indulgence and lack of concern for others exert opposite influences. "People are nourished by other people," said Wolf.[11]

It is important to note that this was a golden age in Roseto. Life changed for the children of the immigrants. Those under thirty left Roseto for better jobs, where life would not be so rigid and traditional. They built large single-family homes and fenced yards, joined country clubs, and attended churches outside of the community. They achieved material success at the expense of the traditional communal values with which they had been raised. Wolf and his colleagues noted the social change in the village was accompanied by increasing health problems. In 1971, the first heart attack death of a person less than age forty-five occurred in Roseto.

People are nourished by other people.

Tackle Your Stress Triggers

We live in America, the land that applauds individuality and self-fulfillment—and retirement. Studies are conclusive that to relieve the stress in our work life we need community and ways to give back to others during our work years, inside and outside the job. Perhaps we need to consider we also need a plan for retirement, when stress changes its presentation. It is dangerous to our health to retire without a plan in hand. If you feel job stress is killing you, consider these statistics:

1. Men and women who retire early (age fifty-five or younger) have a significantly higher early death rate than those retiring at sixty-five.
2. Employees who retired at fifty-five in the higher socioeconomic group had a 20 percent increase in risk of death, whereas early retirees in the lower socioeconomic group had nearly a 60 percent higher risk of death.
3. There was no statistical difference in mortality by socioeconomic status in the group that retired after age sixty-five.
4. The probability of survival for the group who retired at age sixty showed a statistical higher risk of death at ages seventy-five to eighty-three than those who retired at sixty-five.
5. The risk of death was about 80 percent greater for men than it was for women in the low socioeconomic category retiring at age fifty.
6. Those retiring from high-stress leadership positions in business and the military have a significantly higher proportion of deaths within the first two years after retirement than the general working population.
7. The mortality rate improved with increasing age at retirement for people from both high and low socioeconomic groups.[12]

You, unlike our dogs with mange, have the power to do something about your stress. Try keeping a stress inventory if you are having trouble identifying your discomfort at work. For one month write down the situations, events, or people who cause you to have a negative physical, mental, or emotional response. Give a brief description of the situation. Where were you? Who was involved? Describe your reaction. Did you feel frustrated, angry, or

To cope with stress, identify your stress triggers, determine a plan, and implement it.

nervous? Think through your options. The best way to cope with stress on the job or in retirement is to identify its roots and try to find a way to change the circumstances causing it.

Take note of these suggestions to balance your work life with life outside the job:

- *"Get a life"* isn't just a statement for the buzz-off person. It's an important bit of advice for all of us. Having purpose outside of work, such as hobbies, relationships, and a way to give back to others, keeps work life in perspective. All work and no play not only makes you one-sided, it destroys a bit of your spirit. The laughter leaves.

- *Set realistic expectations and deadlines.* "I do the work that three others did before me" is not a positive statement for your health. Overload is costly. Even if you are a superman, something is lost in the process, and more often than not it is your lightness and joy.

- *Organize.* Why feel under the gun and behind the eight ball because you refuse to organize your priorities, schedule, and stuff?

- *Be flexible.* The tenuous balance between work and home life requires juggling.

- *Deal with the reality of your job.* Some things can be changed, some things might change, and some things will never change.

- *Let it go.* Hanging on to the past helps no one. Refuse to spin around issues.

- *Build your team.* You can do it alone, but you can't do it alone and be healthy.

- *Recognize your opportunities to make a difference.*

146

Dancing in the Tension

The Roseto Effect is the key to staying healthy in the work world. It's not hard work that kills you. Many people work hard, live under harsh circumstances, and live long lives. Work isn't a culprit; it is a gift.

If anyone knew hard work and challenges in the workplace, it was J. W. Marriott. Marriott was an American entrepreneur and businessman, and founded the Marriott Corporation, the parent company of one of the world's largest hospitality, hotel chains, and food services companies. His responsibilities and demands were ever constant as the business grew from his first A&W root beer stand to a major hotel/restaurant corporation. Marriott was an energetic worker and rarely rested. He ate, lived, breathed, and dreamed about how to improve his company, personally inspecting every establishment at least four times a year, even when the corporation grew to include hundreds of restaurants and hotels. His son, Bill Jr., remembers that his father's managers

> never knew what time of day or night he'd show up at the kitchen door and go bird-dogging almost at a half-run through the kitchen, the pantries, the storage rooms, the refrigerators, the restaurant itself, running a finger over the shelves to check for dust, checking under tables and in the cutlery drawers, checking the ranges, the storage rooms, the trays about to be served, sampling the root beer and raising the [roof] if everything wasn't spotless, neat, clean, bright, polished, done efficiently, done well . . . yet his employees loved him because . . . Dad paid a lot of attention and tender loving care to the hourly workers. When they were sick, Dad went to see them. When they were in trouble, he got them out of trouble. He created family loyalty.[13]

Marriott is a classic example of the Roseto Effect. His life was filled with stress. When he was thirty-five, after his medical team diagnosed him with malignant cancer of the lymph nodes, they gave him a prognosis of six months to live. At age fifty-five, J. W. Marriott had his first major heart attack. His doctors advised him for the sake of his health to decrease his workload and turn over some of the responsibilities to others. It took five more years and increasing health problems before J. W. finally turned over leadership of the Marriott Corporation to his son. He chose to let go of the reins in order to live. Even with a lifetime of stress, Marriott had the right factors to balance and live to the age of eighty-four: love of his work, a sense of being needed, spiritual strength, and a supportive community.

A healthy social and spiritual life counters the negative effects of workplace stress.

Do you have a stressful job? If you want things to be different, perhaps the answer is to refuse to allow your thoughts about your life, work, and co-workers to control your emotions. Remember: it is not what happens to you that causes stress, it is your response to what happens. Anxiety, tension, fear, and anger do not exist independently of you in the world.

Response is a choice. Be more creative than a teapot. It has only one escape valve to blow off steam. You have a bevy of outlets: friends, family, service in your community, hobbies, even just a night off with a good book after a hot shower.

Insights

- Your career and your health depend upon successfully managing stress.
- Stress is directly proportional to how much you care.

- You enable stress by feeling unable.
- To cope with stress, identify your stress triggers, determine a plan, and implement it.
- A healthy social life with family and friends seems to counter the negative effects of workplace stress.

Questions

1. Do you have a healthy social life outside of work?
2. Are you involved in your community life?
3. Is either your work life or personal life out of balance?
4. If so, are you willing to make changes if your health is as at-risk as the statistics indicate?
5. What keeps you from addressing the factors that cause you stress in your job?

14

When Dealing with Emotions, Do the Outrageous

An eye for an eye makes the whole world blind.

Mahatma Gandhi

There was an employee in the office who was a liar, a documented con, and irresponsible. His supervisor, an experienced manager named Jamie, saw clearly the employee was working the system. He needed to change course. But try as she might to motivate him, his attitude spoke clearly: So what? What can you do? Unfortunately, he was dead-on. He was protected by the company's regulations. He had the power. When the employee made a paper plane out of his biannual evaluation to fly at the supervisor, she declared war on "Mr. Rude-e." She moved his desk next to hers. Bad decision!

The employee continued his irritating behavior. But now instead of observing him from afar, Jamie had him right under her nose. Not good. Desperate times called for desperate measures. In this case, it was a call to me. It was clear she needed to do something outrageous, or at the very least something unusual. Jamie needed to check her spiraling emotions at the door, walk around the block, and come back into the office. Splinters were festering in her spirit, infecting her attitude and judgment.

Dwelling on the negative simply contributes to its power.

I recognized this supervisor as an incredibly talented manager who needed a new approach with Mr. Rude-e. I asked if she ever watched the television series *Monk*. Tony Shaloub plays Adrian Monk, who is a compulsively neat and orderly nutcase with an incredible skill in detective work. His "problem," compulsiveness, helps him detect the slightest irregularity. I suggested to Jamie that her problem, Mr. Rude-e, might provide her with one of her most important business lessons. Caring about the company, Jamie wanted this employee to get off his buns and do his work. Nothing wrong with that! But she had become compulsive, like Monk, wrapped around the employee. The rule when interacting with employees who fly paper airplanes: *take emotion out of the game.*

Don't Let the Airplanes—or Flies—Distract You

I shared a personal lesson with Jamie that I use to pull myself back to the core issue when emotion wants to center me on distractions. My first interview after the publication of *Sunrise Tomorrow: Coping with the Death of a Child* was an hour-long live radio program. An hour is a long time for instant answers and quick sound bites, especially when the night before the interview our family arrived home from a week of vacation at Disney World. From Mickey Mouse to death and dying is a long trek, so I spent most of the night making cheat sheets on topics the host might cover: What was it like to lose a child? Were friends helpful? Did I believe in prayer? What would I suggest to others living through a similar experience? How did my family cope?

The morning of the interview I bustled our children off to school, kissed my husband good-bye, and with cheat sheets in hand went to a room walled off from outside distractions. I needed to be centered and calm. Pauses in radio interviews are pregnant. People listening antici- pate answers; seconds stretch. I sat on the floor beside the phone, spreading the sheets around me. Ten minutes until airtime. As I bowed my head to ask God's insights and peace, a fly flew by, hum- ming, bumping into mirrors, and attacking the windows like a kamikaze pilot. I tried to ignore it. I tried to stay calm through its diving assaults, but when it landed in my hair, the quiet was gone.

If your attention is focused on the fly, open the door.

I became centered on killing the fly. With my shoe in hand, I hit the mirrors and walls with no success at doing more than ir- ritating the fly. I knew I could not listen to that fly for an hour as I talked. I needed a new maneuver. What about simply opening the door? The fly was happy to leave. I had one minute to pull myself together before the phone rang.[1]

The flies in our lives create these reactions:

- Catch our attention
- Become an irritation
- Shift our focus
- Become a compulsion
- Offer an excuse for failure

"Paper airplanes and flies add a surprise element to the workplace," I told Jamie. "Such actions seem to come out of the blue to set our emotions on fire. Ignited, emotions whirlpool reactions." Jamie nodded, but seemed puzzled. "I didn't recognize how wrapped I was around Rude-e until his paper plane set me on fire," she said. "By the time I recognized my plan added to the chaos, everyone was on edge."

Staying centered, appreciating different approaches and ideas, and refusing to spin off when someone else's behavior affects us is incredibly difficult. We are pulled into the fray by our need to get ahead, the desire to be praised, or the fear of losing our opportunities. What someone else does in the workplace affects us! Still, each of us is responsible for not only our actions, but also our reactions. Emotions are signals that alert us to act; unfortunately, they don't tell us how.

I explained to Jamie that keeping emotions under control was crucial to handling problems at work. The difficulty is emotions are sneaky. In slow-building circumstances, emotions start pushing quietly. They gently nag, then quietly build up power. Before you realize it, they are demanding action that may be way out of line. It's as if the problem fed them Geritol, creating such strength that reason is locked out. It is absolutely crucial, when dealing with company problems, to get your emotions under control.

Jamie admitted that though her emotions were stacking, it was the plane surprise that pushed reason aside. Likewise, a simple determined action, such as opening the door to let the fly out, puts reason back in control. To get back in the driver's seat:

1. Calm yourself. Don't yell what you are thinking.
2. Immediately address the issue with a "feeling" that you plan to discuss: "I am very discouraged by . . . I am surprised that . . . I am sure you have a reason for what just happened . . ."

3. Sit down with the offender. He may be a valued, needed asset to the company, as well as someone you like or respect.

4. Listen to his version of the problem in this evaluation stage.

5. Take appropriate action. If the problem is small enough, address it and move on. If it cannot be overlooked or is likely to happen again, you must consider that this person represents the company and is a reflection of your leadership.

> *Emotions are signals that alert us to act; unfortunately, they don't tell us how.*

Do what you must to stop the problem, even if it means surgery instead of rubbing salve on the wounds.

6. By all means, document the encounter and its resolution.

Emotions Are Flighty

Emotions can be corralled. By focusing on the positives, especially in difficult encounters, objectivity slowly pulls recalcitrant emotions into the fold. The emotions calm and fall into alignment. I told Jamie two more thoughts that spin off analogies, which I use to help pull my emotions back into control when they are bouncing off the planes or flies.

Paul Bradshaw interviewed Rick Warren, the author of *The Purpose-Driven Life* and pastor of Saddleback Church in California. Bradshaw asked Rev. Warren how he was holding up with all his responsibilities in the midst of his wife's struggle through cancer treatments.

Rev. Warren said that until his wife's cancer he looked at life as a series of experiences that either put him on the mountaintop where he felt alive and filled with joy, or left him in the valley where darkness seemed to cover his spirit. His wife's battle with cancer caused him to rethink his analogy. Life was more like being on a railroad track. One rail was the crisis: the debilitating chemical treatments and potential death of his wife; the other rail was the special blessings: a friend bringing food, a positive letter, an opportunity, or an unexpected call. He stated that he found by focusing on the rail of blessings, the health issues were still tough, but his family's ability to handle them was bolstered.[2]

> The good news is that emotions have only the strength you give them.

Like Jamie, we all have to cope with people whose attitudes and behaviors threaten to derail us. Yet, as our train keeps chugging along, on the other rail will be someone who supports us, encourages us, and offers us a tiny respite. Jamie nodded, "Throughout this time, there have been co-workers who have been very supportive and are dependable. I can see where focusing on the many positives could help me be less centered on the tactics of a Rude-e."

This Too Shall Pass

Sometimes I find myself calming spinning emotions by saying the phrase "this too shall pass." The first time the phrase appeared in literature was in the works of Persian Sufi poet Attar, whose fable is of a powerful king who asks his assembled wise men to create a ring capable of making him happy when he is sad or sad when he is happy. After deliberation, the sages hand him a simple ring with the words "This too will pass" etched into the gold to remind the king that all is but for a moment.[3]

Jamie suggested, "I bet the king was manic-depressive, swinging and spiraling in emotion! I may not have a mental issue, but I definitely am dealing with problems that drive me to distraction.

If I center on the thought that whatever I am coping with is just for the moment, it would seem less compelling."

Jamie seemed far more in control when I left. She promised to call me when she decided what to do about Mr. Rude-e. She did! I could hear the excitement in her voice. "We won!" she said. "We?" I queried. "Yes. I sat down with Rude-e after you left and, instead of telling him he was missing the mark, I did it—the outrageous thing! I asked if there were any other area in our company that would suit him better. It was like I opened a floodgate. Bottom line: he was incredibly bored, unhappy, and felt stuck. I moved him immediately. Now we are both 'unstuck.'"

> *Your calm allows you to do the outrageous: design a plan to do the possible in what feels like an impossible situation.*

Emotions love control. The good news is that emotions have only the strength you give them. Knowing no one can make anyone do anything keeps emotions from building up in intensity as they pound on a closed door. Instead, your calm allows you to do the outrageous: design a plan to do the possible in what feels like an impossible situation.

Insights

- Dwelling on the negative simply contributes to its power.
- Emotions have only the strength you give them.
- Respect your emotions when they talk to you.
- Sometimes you need to bite your tongue until the moment is right to address the issue.
- Open the door and let the flies out!
- Knowing no one can make anyone do anything keeps emotions from mushrooming; instead, your calm allows you to

do the outrageous: design a plan to do the possible in what feels like an impossible situation.

- Get the emotions back in the corral.
- Hang loose, because "this too shall pass."

Questions

1. Why is it so difficult to control emotions that spin around situations at work?
2. Do you feel you can change the way you react to a difficult person in your workplace without losing face?
3. What techniques can you use to keep from being controlled by someone's negative behavior?
4. Are you willing to risk talking with the person around whom you are spinning about the problem?

15

Let It Go

When you forgive, you in no way change the past—but you do change the future.

Most of us brush away the gnat problems at work. It is hardly worth the effort to hang on to those pesky issues. But there are other more momentous issues that cause us to circle the drain. I recall a man who stood up at a conference to ask, "Can you help me?" He had been figuratively struck by lightning and felt burned to a crisp.

"I worked in a major chemical company," he said. "After being warned by the CEO that my division was on the chopping block if we didn't pull up production, we pulled in the reins and went from near bottom to the top. But he said, 'Too late!' My team then proposed to buy the sector. We had the loans, the know-how, the staff, and the drive to make it go. The big dog shook his head. 'Sorry,' he said. 'It's not personal. We need a loss feeder for our bottom line.' It was personal to the thirty-six of us who lost our jobs. I know he had to produce or his head would be the next to roll, but at the very least he owed me a sincere apology. I put years of effort into that job!"

There is no denying that there are times an apology is due and might put salve on wounds. Yet this distressed chap was wrong to believe an apology would erase his pain. Forgiveness is a choice to free *yourself*, and to find lessons instead of bitterness. Preconditions are salve, not healing. No victim ever feels someone's apology is enough to make up for the injustice; no guilty person will be freed by someone saying "it's all right." A condition that must be met gives power to the other person. If he meets the condition, you are forced to stuff your feelings; if he refuses, you must nurse the feeling of resentment or guilt. The problem is that even though forgiving is better, stuffing and spinning are easier.

> *Letting go should never be held hostage to a precondition.*

Pebbles in the Heart

There is a story that is far too common, told with slightly different variables through the lives of many around us. The story begins with a baby, a baby born to parents who were far too old for another child. The father cursed the day baby Christofer was born, a child who would end his plans for retirement and freedom. The mother was filled with resentment at being handcuffed to a needy infant who would thwart her wishes. His older brothers unmercifully teased Christofer and often told him what hardship he caused his family. The child was a nuisance, and a constant hindrance to their plans. Never a day passed that the little boy did not cower for fear his father would beat him for some grievance, his mother would accuse him with her spiteful eyes, or his brothers would ridicule his efforts.

Despite Christofer's disparaging home life, he was so gifted in mind, manner, and looks that he easily found work, and seemed to be one marked by destiny to rise quickly to the top in his career. There was only one problem: authority. Whenever someone above him in the chain of command issued a demand, he remembered his father's commands and resentment filled his soul. Though he was good at hiding his thoughts, with each feeling of anger a pebble fell into his heart.

The business community, knowing the young man's difficult childhood, praised him, saying, "What a strong man Christofer is to forgive his parents and brothers for such a difficult childhood."

Through the years, as Christofer climbed to the company's top position, he slowly became hard and cold as resentments stacked. It could be seen in his eyes and felt in his attitude. Associates no longer invited him for lunch. Laughter and joy left his soul. In a particularly contentious moment, he used his power to squelch an employee who dared to share a contrary thought. Another pebble filled the last remaining space of light in his body. In that meeting Christofer turned to stone.

True forgiveness allows growth from the past and prevents stones from forming in the heart. Forgiving is not forgetting. No one forgets something that punches their emotions. Forgiveness stores the act in your mind's computer, filed under "Lesson Learned." Though the hurt may occasionally surface, it no longer stings. If someone had reminded a more forgiving Christofer of his harsh childhood, he simply would have regarded it as a time from which he learned to handle difficulty. He would have been grateful for life and sorrowful that his family missed the opportunity to feel the love of another child.

Business crises, just like personal calamities, are notorious for wrecking lives. The man who spoke up in the seminar was stewing over an injustice at his workplace that happened years ago, even knowing that what had been done was part of the effort to keep the business viable. Understanding *why* doesn't justify a hurt to the one aching. It is interesting to note that every major feud in history has begun over business problems. Job-related problems, like those in a family, don't end as you walk out the door. They are taken home, tended, and brought back each day. It is personal when performance is criticized, a job is downsized, a promotion is denied, or co-workers form cliques without you. So what are you to do if you are dealing with an issue that is consuming your thoughts? There are two possibilities: harbor or process.

Internal peace within difficult situations is the result of a choice: to process instead of harbor.

The Hatfields and McCoys harbored. This infamous mountain-family feud lasted sixty-seven years, from 1863 to 1930. The feud was fueled by economic and political reasons more than the folk-loric version of lost love and pigs. The extreme dislike was between farm neighbors in the remote Appalachian Tug Valley of Kentucky and West Virginia. The Hatfields of West Virginia were more prosperous than their neighbors. They began a successful timber business and wanted the McCoys' forest land. The McCoys refused to sell, so the Hatfields took the issue to court. The courts sided with the Hatfields and gave them the ownership of 5,000 acres of land on the Kentucky side of the Tug River, which the McCoys claimed. During the Civil War, when Devil Anse Hatfield sided with the Confederacy and Rand McCoy with the Union, both felt their properties were in danger. A tit-for-tat aggression, with both sides stealing hogs, horses, and hides, elevated the clans' hostilities to increased violence. Devil Anse's nephew was killed in a drunken brawl; in return, his gang killed two of the McCoy boys. In all, twelve Hatfields and McCoys were killed during the sixty-seven-year feud.

The Hatfields and McCoys carried their can't-get-along issues to the extreme, but it isn't easy for any of us to let go. All of us hang on way too long when we feel someone has taken our hog, stolen our hides, or ridden off on our horse.

The man struggling to forgive his ex-boss knew he needed to move on. He just didn't know how. It is a process, not an overnight "forget it" event when someone hurts you, either intentionally or unintentionally. The choice either to move on and forgive or hang on and harbor changes your life. Forgiving sets you free; harboring wraps you in bitterness.

Freeing Yourself from the Baggage

Please hear me clearly. Forgiving someone does not require you to continue a negative relationship. It simply frees you from simmering and stewing in the past. It arms you with detachment to work with screwed-up people without becoming as messed up and as difficult as they are.

Forgiveness happens when a mental lightbulb turns on: *She may drive me crazy, but I am the one who carries the baggage everywhere I go.* Forgiving gets rid of the baggage. It turns mere survival into victorious living as it cuts you loose from the power of the difficult person in your life, your desire for revenge, or your guilt over wrongdoing. It is a determination to not let what someone else did destroy you, regardless of how you are affected. The sad reality is that, in far too many cases, ten years after a serious breakdown in

Forgiving is a process.

a relationship such as divorce or a broken business alliance, one of the parties is still carrying around the grudge and hurt.

The 1986 movie *The Mission* poignantly addressed the issue of forgiveness, the letting go of significant injustice. The story depicts the mission efforts of the Jesuits with the Guarani Indians who live above the spectacular Iguzau Falls in South America. Robert de Niro plays mercenary and slaver Rodrigo Medoza, who makes his living kidnapping Guaranis and other indigenous people and selling them to the nearby plantation. Medoza has a personal crisis, repents of his deeds, and seeks absolution of his guilt by wrapping himself in chains and a satchel full of the armor and weapons he once used to capture the Indians. In one of the movie's most memorable scenes, Medoza has stumbled repeatedly, and falls to the edge of a precipice. With the weight of the satchel and chains there is little hope of him regaining a foothold to climb from the edge. At that moment a Guarani Indian who has escaped from slavery steps from behind a bush with a machete held over his head. The audience gasps as the blade comes down. Instead of seeking revenge, the Indian cuts through the chains, freeing the satchel to plummet over the falls. Medoza is able to stand. The Guarani closed the book on an unjust chapter in his life. He let the past go, freeing himself to move forward and do right. He chose to be responsible for his own actions and responses, not to be bound by someone else's wrong acts or captive to his past as Mendoza was.[1] To free yourself requires a decision to put down the burden of hurt that locks you in chains and encumbers your climb up the mountains.

> *Forgiving someone does not require you to continue a negative relationship, but it does demand you get rid of the baggage.*

The Attribute of the Strong

Gandhi told his nation that being able to forgive is the attribute of the *strong*, not the *naive*. We are meant to learn, to grow wise from experience. We are naive to overlook wrong, thinking it won't happen again. It is not mercy to allow someone to get away with hurtful acts that lock her into behavior that destroys others and rewards her transgression. Seeking justice is healthy and responsible, as opposed to revenge, which is payback, a settling of scores, a vengeance that locks us into war games. Justice requires someone be held responsible for their actions, even as we acknowledge we are not responsible for his or her wrongdoing.

Nothing annoys an enemy more than your forgiving him. *You lose your fear of his actions; he loses his power to tie you in knots.* Perhaps you will find these proven methods helpful in overcoming the normal, natural feelings that want to spin off injustice:

- Refuse to take responsibility for someone else's wrong action. Each of us is responsible for what we do. Someone arguing "You made me do it!" doesn't make it so!

- Acknowledge that the wrong affects you, but determine not to let it cocoon you.

Seeking justice is healthy; seeking revenge is not.

- Feel sorrow that someone is so thoughtless about how his or her actions hurt others that they break relationship opportunities by their misdeeds.

- Pray that you can release the hurt.

- Pray for the person. Prayer helps you care "in spite of," rather than "because of."

- Know your limits. When you are close to going off the edge, do whatever is necessary to regain control: leave the situation, talk yourself down, or say outright, "Excuse me, but what you are doing is wrong. It is unacceptable."

- Seek justice, not revenge.
- Forgive, knowing it is your gift to yourself.
- Recognize that forgiving someone does not require you to continue a negative relationship.

Sometimes the hardest person to forgive is yourself. The reason forgiving yourself is so difficult is that you grieve, longing for the lost relationship and lost time. We hang on, wishing we could erase a misdeed, hoping we will hear the words "You are forgiven." We hobble *self*, trying to make up for the wrong. If you have blown it, you have the same choice as when you face someone else who has injured you: harbor or process. Processing frees you to acknowledge the wrong and change direction. It cannot be dependent upon whether the injured party forgives you. That is their choice and their battle. Even understanding *why* doesn't excuse or justify a wrong. Count on the guilt occasionally surfacing. It is a wish that you could undo what was done. You can't. Only when you use your failure to learn the importance of doing the right thing, regardless of any excuse, will any good come from a misdeed.

In the *Peanuts* cartoon, Lucy is in the batter's box. Charlie Brown is anxious and counsels her on how to swing, knowing Lucy always misses the ball when she bats. This time the pitch comes straight to her bat. There seems no way Lucy can miss. There is excitement in the air. Lucy swings and the ball whizzes on by to the catcher's mitt. "What happened?" cries Charlie. Lucy shrugged. "The past got in my eyes." Sad! Don't let the issues in the past destroy the joy in your present.

Insights

- Letting go is not forgetting; it is forgiving.
- Forgiving cannot have preconditions.
- Forgiving allows you to handle difficult relationships at work without becoming screwed-up.
- Internal peace within difficult situations is the result of a choice to process instead of harbor.
- Letting go, not forgetting, leads to joy.
- Resolve not to allow someone else's behavior to destroy your joy.
- Seeking justice is different from seeking revenge.

Questions

1. Why is letting go so difficult?
2. What is the difference between forgetting and forgiving?
3. How can you prevent being tread upon if you don't keep your guard up?
4. What is the difference between justice and revenge?
5. Why is forgiving so hard?

16

It's Time to Say I'm Sorry

In taking revenge a man is but even with his enemy;
but in passing it over, he is superior.

Francis Bacon

Gracious people know how to accept responsibility for their mistakes. They know, because from the time they were knee-high to a grasshopper they were forced to hug and make up after intentionally—or unintentionally—doing something wrong. You know the drill: you blew it, apologize. But that isn't easy when you are working with people who burn bridges, take but don't give, are in it for self, and may even be unscrupulous. Or perhaps they aren't bad guys. They just have their own agenda or are flying on their own wavelength, doing their own thing regardless of the needs of their team. What if, being the considerate person you are, you say, "I'm sorry," and they just look at you, unforgiving—or even worse, not caring?

"I can tell you about that," a comptroller of a small company said to me. "We needed space for an additional accounting clerk's desk in our department's crowded and overutilized office. The only space available was the protected baby of our uptight, compulsive bookkeeper, who used it for his alphabetized collection of catalogs and product manuals. I requested multiple times that the books be moved to the company library so the precious space could be used for our new employee. Finally I took matters into my own hands. The books were moved to the library while the employee was out to lunch. He was furious! His tirade made it crystal clear I had crossed his battle line.

"I attempted to cool his rage by justifying the move, reminding him of the multiple requests and the new employee's need. He was not appeased! I was sorry for the chaos and tried to apologize, saying I was sorry, but he interrupted me, saying, 'You certainly are sorry. You are the sorriest excuse for a manager I have ever worked with.' His comeback was lightning fast and caught me by such surprise that I started laughing. I said, 'That was really quick, I'm impressed!' He huffed off with a burr under his saddle. The confrontation stopped but the tension was not eased."

Dealing with unmanageable people requires the wisdom of Solomon. You are right that your job description does not require pampering, nurturing, or babysitting the inconsiderate, thoughtless, mindless, unfair, or competitive with their multitude of quirky behaviors. You are not required to be best friends with those at work. But when tension is palpable and splinters are festering, you must deal with the reality that though you shouldn't have to put up with crud, you will have to address the issue with tact before a scrimmage escalates to full-out battle.

You need perspective. Pull back. Ask yourself: Why am I so emotional about this issue? Is my manner helping or escalating the problem? What works? What doesn't work? What is my next step? You may not be able to get someone else to figuratively move his books, but you can control what you do. And, when you blow it, you need to figure out how to hug and apologize.

Apologizing is emotional if your focus is your belly button. Belly button focus asks: Why should I apologize to someone who complicates my life with her irrational behavior? Why should I, when:

- It feels like I am saying you are right.
- My actions weren't intentional.
- I don't want to grovel.
- It feels like I'm admitting wrong when I wouldn't have done it if you hadn't . . .
- I don't want to let you off the hook.
- It gives you ammunition to gun me down and a hammer to bash me.
- It is an admission that I am part of the problem.
- Time will take care of it.

Types of Apologies

The most common apology is a **calm the water apology**. Such apologies keep tension from escalating. It says, "I care. I'm sorry you are unhappy. I am sorry the customer berated you. I'm sorry I misunderstood your directions. I'm sorry you have been on the telephone line waiting for a real person for thirty minutes." "I care" apologies dampen the vent syndrome, the whirlwind of anger that escalates when someone feels unheard or unfairly treated. You attempt to de-escalate the tension that may volcano, even when you are not personally responsible. Such apologies empower you to be objective, rather than being entangled or decimated by someone's barrage.

Wouldn't it be nice if "I care" apologies always worked? The comptroller's apology was an attempt to calm the water. If it helps, you feel relief. You don't have to put up with a volley of verbal bullets. The hope is that an apology will assuage potential bedlam.

An **I take responsibility for what I did wrong apology** is for you to do what is right, regardless of another's response. The goal is freedom. The person who apologizes takes personal responsibility for his actions, freeing him to no longer cower, hide, or blame. It unties emotions that want to circle the wagons. An apology acknowledges that "no one made me lose it; my actions and responses belong to me." A sincere apology frees the one who has done wrong and offers the injured party the opportunity to let go of hurt or anger. Apologizing, like forgiving, is an inside job. The past no longer sits beside you on the judgment bench.

This apology allows no tagalongs. You may not attempt to justify what you did by what the other person did. If you do, your apology is dead in the water. You won't be freed and they won't even consider letting it go or changing. In fact, tagalongs blow the tension off the barometer. Keep it simple and pinpointed to the wrong. "I'm sorry for . . ."

An **in your face apology** is a backhanded way to slap the one to whom you offer the tongue-in-cheek verbiage. It says clearly, "I'm the saint who is apologizing even though you caused the problem." You know this apology; you used it plenty as a child when a parent or a teacher forced you to apologize. Remember how your eyes rolled as your words and your anger joined hands to let it be known, "I'm apologizing, but you deserved it." It does nothing for anyone—the other person or yourself.

Probably all of us have experienced such a disingenuous apology, one that was forced, insincere, or cutting. An insincere apology is very hard to disguise. So if you are going to apologize, do not do it out of obligation. The apology may appease the one hurt (if he doesn't see through the insincerity), but it doesn't free the one who did the wrong. An apology should clearly say, "I am sorry for my wrong."

A **politician apology** is an attempt to hide the truth. Failure to take responsibility for your own actions, no matter how painful, adds to the wrong and speaks volumes about character. Nobody wants to be caught with his or her hand in the cookie jar, but if that is the case, fess up to it. Ultimately, the person you must live with is yourself. It is far better to live with the knowledge you are mature enough to acknowledge your responsibility for a wrong than to watch as, piece by piece, the truth comes out. The end result of hidden guilt can be likened to a worm wiggling in the rain-soaked ground, trying to get air. It's heartrending to watch.

Wrong thought apologies are killers: killers of relationships, hopes, dreams, and jobs. Thoughts are thoughts. They flash through the mind like lightning in a storm. They only become dangerous if allowed to play like a broken record or move from the mind to the mouth. A building inspector was appalled by his assistant's apology for her lustful thoughts toward him. He was embarrassed and fearful that her comments might be shared with other staff members. Maybe she thought he would be flattered, but the comment was not only inappropriate, it cost her the job.

False humility apologies are bogus. Apologies become meaningless if they roll like marbles in all directions: "I'm sorry I touched your desk. I'm sorry I didn't offer to get you coffee. I'm sorry. I'm sorry." Such apologies are born from low self-esteem or a one-upmanship. If an apology is only to project the image of humility, it is blatantly wrong and demeans a true effort to take responsibility for a wrong.

Inappropriate apologies are just that: uncalled for and incorrect. Do not apologize for taking a stand against evil or wrongdoing. Anger is justified when the boundaries of safety, decency, and respect are trampled. In fact, at such times to not respond in an effort to stop the behavior is a symptom of mental, emotional, or spiritual disorder. You can be sorry if you overreacted, and express your intention to not lose control again, but that assumes the other person understands and respects the boundaries. "I apologized for losing my temper with my boss, but I finally told him I could not work overtime anymore this month. It would be crazy to lose my marriage because I have a workaholic boss." "I am sorry I seemed curt when you appeared at my home with work that you wanted done after the workday. I am happy to work diligently while I am at the office, but after hours are mine."

A **self-flagellation apology** is crippling. If you feel inadequate, untalented, or a failure, what good is an apology? Of course, you are sorry you aren't a superman or superwoman, but if you aren't happy about your state, do something about it. To apologize for such is like hanging your head for someone to pat it and allow "poor little you" to continue feeling like a victim. An acquaintance wrote a blanket apology to his fraternity: "In 1990 I took a camera someone brought to the dining area. I'm writing to all of you, my fraternity brothers, to ask that you please forgive me." This apology would have carried more weight if the repentant brother had added: "Call me so I can purchase you another camera." He was on a penance journey, attempting to clear his inside problem by a blanket apology.

If a physician were treating a patient, she wouldn't load the patient up with every medicine in the cabinet. She would do the footwork necessary to discover the right drug for the patient's specific need. Perhaps in our personal arena we need to follow the same approach: when there is doubt, narrow the field to find the right target for an apology.

Be careful with **confession apologies**. A professional counselor or priest/minister/rabbi are good choices if the inside alarm of guilt is driving you to fess up. Too often a confession is made to the victim, whose self-esteem is blown out of the water by the unexpected bombshell. Sometimes it slips out to the media, who relish a juicy public confession and plaster it on the airwaves and magazine covers without any consideration of the company, family, or loved ones hurt by the broadcast. I wonder at times if such a confession is a subconscious attempt to put the onus of guilt on the victim, to sweep the junk onto someone else's doorstep or to somehow justify the wrong: "Gee, I am sorry I took money from the cash drawer. I meant to bring it back as soon as I got back on my feet." "I'm sorry. It didn't mean anything. I just got so lonely on the road."

When there is doubt as to whom you should apologize, narrow the field to find the right target before you do so.

A good general rule for a confession is simple: confess if it will help the other person and strengthen the relationship. Use discernment if the confession will simply relieve your guilt while layering a coat of anguish onto the one who hears your declaration of guilt.

Blanket apologies are debatable. One might argue that even though you deeply regret an injustice, to apologize for such when you did not support the action in any way smells of political correctness and hypocrisy. But what about the argument that an apology might put salve on a wound? There are times that a simple statement of sorrow is salve to cover a victim's hurt. A sincere apology that says "I care that you were wounded" can be a key to unlock the bitterness spinning around wrongs—or not. An apology throws the ball back to the injured party to determine whether he wants to hang on to the hurt or free himself. Reconciliation is a two-way street and only those apologies that are accepted have a healing effect.

Issues abound that we may not condone. The question is, by saying nothing are we in complicity? What about the co-worker unfairly fired when new management determines to get rid of the old to make way for the new? Was it fair that the female co-worker was shuffled to another department or let go for a fling with her boss, but the boss was not? What about the multiple jobs in the tech corridors of our cities that repetitively hire employees as temporary staff to fulfill their contract in order to not be obligated for full-time employee benefit packages? What about the unreasonable demands made on employees that are justified by saying, "If you want to get to the top, do it; if not, quit!" There are many wrongs in our world, and we cannot correct them all. Consider these three guides in determining when to apologize:

1. Apologize for your own actions if, intentionally or unintentionally, someone was hurt or wronged.
2. Offer an "I care" blanket apology when appropriate: "I'm sorry you lost your job," or "I'm sorry that the boss is unreasonable," and possibly even go the next step to address the grievance through the proper channels in your company. However, be thoughtful. Becoming an adult's "defense attorney" is often an inappropriate action. Like a table, no one is balanced until he stands on his own legs.
3. Do not hesitate to apologize for wrong actions of others to children and those too captive to recognize abuse. The fact

that another views the hurt as wrong may help an injured party appropriately evaluate actions that can be couched in "you deserve this" or "it's your fault" justification.

Essential Elements of an Apology

It is important to consider six essential elements in an effective apology game plan: location, timing, preparation, focus, presentation, and making right the wrong.

Location

Choose a neutral location, one that does not make either person feel uncomfortable or overpowered. Choose a place where there will be few distractions and the conversation will not be overheard. An apology is personal and should be made to the person who has been offended. If the person has been publicly humiliated by your actions, it is wise to ask his or her permission before correcting the act with others. No cell phones allowed.

> *A sincere apology frees the person who has done wrong and offers the injured party the opportunity to let go of the hurt or anger.*

Timing

The sooner the better! The old adage, "Never let the sun go down on your anger," is a wise injunction. Simmering anger grows exponentially. However, don't rush an apology. Recognize and bow to cool-down styles. Some people are able to apologize or receive an apology immediately after a hurt; others need to lower their walls before either can be more than just mouthed words. When you do apologize, make sure there will be plenty of time to talk out the issues. Whatever you do, refuse to counter accusations with justifications or finger-pointing. A few simple ways to address incorrect statements: "I'm sorry. I don't think that," "That is not my belief," or "I did not mean to give that impression."

Preparation

Apologies flow from accepting responsibility for one's actions. They do not have to be poetic or perfect. People want to see a change in your attitude and/or beliefs, or at the very least an acknowledgment that you respect them. Be specific, not general. Simple is best. "I am sorry I did . . . I was wrong." "I am sorry you were hurt." "I intend to make amends by . . ." "I do not want to do this again. I hope I have learned . . ." Prepare your apology to cover these six areas, in this order:

1. Acknowledgment of a specific wrong
2. Acknowledgment of your responsibility
3. Acknowledgment of your sorrow over the other's hurt
4. Intention to make amends
5. Intention to not repeat behavior
6. Focus on lessons you learned

Focus and Presentation

Center on your own actions. Don't get sidetracked into justifications. Be simple, to the point, with no hint of self-gain or self-protection. Your caring should be evident in your words, gestures, and expressions. Be cautious. Wait out interruptions. Accept full responsibility for your part in the wrong and offer no justification, even if you are attacked. "I did wrong. I'm sorry."

Making Amends

Apologies sometimes require that you make amends to the person you harmed or to others affected by the wrong. For instance, if you were promoted after taking credit for a subordinate's work, you need to admit it, not by suggesting to the one you shafted that you will "take care of him" once you move upstairs, but rather by addressing the discrepancy with the promotion guru. The scenarios are exhaustless. Guilt will be your inside alarm to do something to correct problems you knowingly or unknowingly caused.

> *Guilt is an inside alarm that signals the need to apologize and, if possible, make amends.*

When an Apology Isn't Going to Happen

Sometimes no apology will break through the walls built against you. "You blew it. . . . You are too late . . . too wrong . . . too terrible . . ." The price paid for doing a wrong is an "eggs-perience." You know how it goes: "Humpty Dumpty sat on a wall. Humpty Dumpty had a great fall. . . . All the king's horses and all the king's men couldn't put Humpty together again." Sad for Humpty Dumpty; good for you that you aren't an egg! Pick up your pieces and go forward. Repeated apologies become begging. Begging kills all hope for rekindling a relationship!

What do you do if it's too late? Death, health problems, politics, moves, even resistance may not allow you to apologize. You might find it helpful to write a letter to the person, even knowing it cannot be delivered. Write your thoughts, your regrets, and what you are going to do with the lesson learned. Thank the person for being a catalyst to your growth. Read your apology, then burn it. The act is a tangible symbol that helps you let go of a sad chapter in your life.

Victor Frankl, an Austrian neurologist, psychiatrist, and Holocaust survivor, wrote *Man's Search for Meaning*. In this small book he vividly describes the overwhelming need to apologize felt by the survivors of the death camps of WWII. Each survivor donned a mantle of shame, knowing that their survival had required hoarding and self-preservation at the expense of others. They were overwhelmed by the knowledge that, when push came to shove, they were as guilty as some of their guards in their failure to stand up for their suffering comrades.

Repeated apologies become begging. Begging kills relationships!

Frankl developed an emphasis on "first days." "Today is the first day of the rest of my life." First days don't require that your past be perfect or that you have it all figured out in the present; they just require your conscious decision to overpower the internal voices that want to pull you down by focusing on the times you failed, the times you did wrong, or the times you did not care. It is true that humbling yourself to apologize is much more difficult than sweeping the problem under the rug, but if you are going to stand as an adult, overcome the inner voice that begs to justify your wrong. Free yourself. Today can be your first day.

Insights

- An apology frees the person who offers it.
- Your actions and responses belong to you.
- Guilt is an inside alarm that signals the need to apologize and, if possible, make amends.
- An apology begins the first day of the rest of your life.
- When there is doubt as to whom you should apologize, narrow the field to find the right target before you do so.

Questions

1. Why is it so hard to say "I'm sorry"?
2. How can you keep justification for your wrong from stopping the apology you need to make?
3. How do you handle the rage if the one to whom you apologize slams you with her anger or hurt?
4. What is stopping you from forgiving—not justifying—the one who owes you an apology?
5. What do you do if you know the person who did you wrong will never acknowledge his guilt?
6. Whom does forgiveness free: the person who apologizes or the person receiving the apology?
7. Why do we continue to wallow in guilt long after we have accepted our responsibility for a wrong?
8. Is it right to apologize for something you did not do, but do regret?

An apology begins the first day of the rest of your life.

17

Touch with Words

The difference between the right word and the almost right word is the difference between lightning and the lightning bug.

Mark Twain

Communication with most people is an art, but with difficult people your words may be misinterpreted regardless of what you say. If you are dealing with screwed-up people at work, it may help you to understand:

- They do not hear what you say.
- They will not follow your logic.
- They believe what they want to believe.
- You cannot change them by trying to change them.

So how do you communicate? If communication is a handshake, a negotiation, a team play, how is it possible with such a person?

It isn't! Not in the usual sense: one person sharing his ideas with another to bring about a compromise, each hoping to broaden the other's understanding and to move toward mutual goals.

A person who is fixated on her own agenda has an almost impenetrable deafness. You won't change her by coddling, spinning off, gossiping, or arguing. Such actions simply add resolve to her patterns.

Words are precious tools and we often take for granted that our words are interpreted and understood as we meant them. You may simply say, "This needs to be done." Your words aren't a personal attack, or a statement implying the individual is not doing his job well. You aren't trying to control or be disrespectful. The task is to be done for the sake of the company, the team, or you. Yet words are filtered. If the filter is askew, your words are interpreted through a fog of suspicion, anger, or a host of webs that can turn a zilch comment into a wedge. (Remember the chapter on personality, behavior, and temperament? Go back and review it.)

The person to whom you are speaking is seeking to read you as much as hear you.

It is interesting that screwed-up people may misinterpret your words, but read your body language clearly. Nature programmed us to read the intentions behind words and actions. So, though someone may misinterpret your words, they rarely miss the pushiness, anger, irritation, or annoyance. They stiffen against criticism lurking behind begrudging agreement. They resent political correctness that puts an arm around their shoulders while body language criticizes their actions. The person to whom you are speaking is seeking to read you as much as hear you. That basic instinct may be helpful to you when you are trying to get a point across.

A supervisor, David, conveyed his dilemma when promoted over an employee who was the former kingpin in that job. Her resentment was tangible. I asked how he handled the situation. He replied that he put his words in a velvet glove over a steel fist. David explained, "This woman had been with the company a quarter of a century, so I felt it might be possible for her to be a valuable asset if she could overcome her negativity. I invited her to sit down and talk. I stayed with the facts. I started by stating positive traits: she knew her job, was good at it, and had an immense influence on the other team members. I stated the obvious: I was the new guy. I asked, "Can you work with me?" I could see a lightbulb turn on. Being a mentor changed her from feeling *under* me to working *with* me. It gave her a way to save face. Yet, she understood clearly that I was onto her game."

Use the sandwich approach.

The manager used the "sandwich approach." He sandwiched his comments, placing a positive comment on each side of a negative one. Using a sandwich approach softens comments that can be interpreted as critical. At the same time, it offers the thorny person an opportunity to see the self-benefit of cooperating, as opposed to continuing behavior that is detrimental. As you approach someone you find problematic, try sandwiching your comments:

- Bread: state something positive about the person.
- Meat: state the negative problem behavior that needs to change.
- Bread: state a specific positive characteristic that would help reach a specific goal.

The How-Tos of Communication with Screwed-Up People

It isn't pleasant trying to get on the same page with someone who doesn't care to be part of the team. Be careful. Words are precious, and once spoken cannot be retracted. Many a man and woman have wished their tongues were glued to the roofs of their mouths after machine-gunning words out of sheer frustration. Force yourself to stay objective and detached when you encounter rebelliousness, disrespect, or neediness. Perhaps the individual is struggling with problems at home, or maybe the problem is a perceived threat at work. Neither gives someone the right to be defensive, mean, noncompliant, or unfair, but suggesting to yourself that there may be legitimate reason for ugly behavior does give you a handle to keep your emotions from firing bullets and a rationale to find the root of the problem.

It is crucial that you stay cool. You lose if you get angry, wail, or beg. In the Bible the walls of Jericho came tumbling down when the Israelites marched in sync around the city and then blew their trumpets. What human would have suggested such a tactic? The way to make a difficult person's walls come tumbling down may be just as illogical. The point is that walls can come down, but you may feel as hopeless as the marching horde of Israelites felt at Jericho. Walls fall when you touch a sensitive cord that breaks through the barrier. It may be as simple as quietly acknowledging the negative behavior and asking if change is possible. It is difficult but possible to find ways that enable words combined with acts to catalyze change.

Stephen Covey, author of *The Seven Habits of Highly Effective People*, suggests beginning with the end in mind.[1] Knee-jerk reactions get us in trouble. In 1945 Branch Rickey, manager of the Brooklyn Dodgers, signed Jackie Robinson for the Dodgers' minor league organization. Branch warned him he would face prejudice, but if he would refuse to react, he might open the door to professional athletics for others of color. Robinson set fielding and batting records for the Dodgers, and was named Major League

Baseball's Rookie of the Year in 1947. He was also named the National League's Most Valuable Player in 1949 and inducted into the Baseball Hall of Fame in 1962. Today Jackie Robinson is revered for his stellar career and character that opened the doors of professional sports to all athletes. When he was asked what was the most difficult part of being in the major league, he responded, "Keeping

Walls can come down.

my cool." You, too, can do more than just succeed in your career if you stay in control of your words and acts. Don't let pride undermine your goal.

Getting through the Plugged Ears

David used the sandwich idea. He wanted to know if I had any other special tactic I found helpful when dealing with difficult people. "Try humor," I suggested. "Humor isn't expected. It surprises! It allows you to distance yourself from emotions that want to tie you up in self-defense and batting-back reactions." Marketing guru Jon Spoelstra suggests that if you are having difficulty getting an idea across, push the envelope. "If people fall down laughing when you present an idea, the idea has a chance of becoming a breakthrough idea. When an idea is so outrageous that it causes people to laugh at the idiocy of it, then it's time to push the envelope and see if the idea can be developed."[2]

Ronald Reagan served two terms as President of the United States, from 1981–89. He was often called the "great communicator" because of his quick wit and storytelling. He also was the oldest person ever elected president, an issue seized upon by his opponent Walter Mondale. In the October 21, 1984 presidential debate, Reagan pushed the envelope with humor and, in doing so, used the smoking gun to his advantage. "I want you to know,"

Reagan said, smiling at his opponent, "that I will not make age an issue of this campaign." Then looking at his audience, he smiled. "I am not going to exploit, for political purposes, my opponent's youth and inexperience."[3]

Choose Your Words Carefully

When speaking with difficult people, there are some key phrases that will keep you from falling into a trap. You don't have to lay out a plan, just a thought or a question, maybe even a story of how something you have done took you down the wrong road. You may say:

- Do you believe that what you are doing will help?
- Is there another way that might be more helpful in getting your point across?
- I appreciate you sharing your view/idea.
- I will consider that.

Combine Kind Acts with Words

I applaud Senator Harold Hughes for his tact and kindness at the national prayer breakfast in Washington, DC, where he was the keynote speaker. Just before he was to address the five hundred guests, a flurried waitress dropped a tray of desserts on him. Amidst apologies and hushed silence, the chagrined waitress tried to wipe the gooey mess off the senator's coat and white shirt. Senator Hughes assured the young woman he was okay, but she was aghast. As she turned to leave, the senator stood, touched the waitress's still-red face, and gently kissed her cheek. The blush disappeared and in its place a smile spread over her face. She left the room, radiant, head erect, without shame. Instead of remembering her disgrace, this young woman would retell the story of the accidental spill, remembering that "Senator Harold Hughes kissed me right there in front of all those people after I dropped cherry cobbler all over him!"

Senator Hughes understood how words help or harm. He knew that sometimes, no matter how well words are communicated, they are not heard. He understood that when gentle words are followed by acts of kindness, the words are heard through walls of anger, guilt, shame, or pain.[4]

> *Words combined with kind acts may break through the communication barrier.*

Echo What Is Being Said

Echoing keeps down the friction. The one who echoes is able to stay more emotionally detached. It keeps blame games from escalating. Listen without editorializing. Don't give away your inner feelings by body language that clearly says "Unbelievable!" or "Ridiculous!"

Use nonconfrontational statements: "Are you saying . . . ?" "I appreciate your concern." "Would you say that again?" "Am I understanding . . . ?" When someone hears their words echoed back, often one of four things happens:

- It doesn't sound quite right, so she tries to adjust her thoughts.
- He quits being so defensive because he feels someone is listening thoughtfully and respectfully.
- Possibly, you recognize some logic in what is being said.
- Feeling your respect, she might consider your logic.

Physicians spend much of their time echoing a patient's words to root out the problem. A difficult patient in a nursing home was certain she was being overdosed with sleeping medication. The physician reviewed the chart, talking to her about each medicine. None of the medicines on her chart had a side affect of drowsiness, but the patient stood her ground. Rather than argue with the patient, the doctor took the chart to the nurse's station to review it against the nurse's chart. Sure enough, the patient was correct. A sleeping pill had been carried over from a previous hospitalization. Fortunately, because the doctor listened and echoed respectfully, he could resolve the problem without getting egg on his face.

Use Praise

Many a hardened soul has been softened by simple praise. You don't have to lie. It should be appropriate to the situation. Try these neutralizing phrases:

- Really? How interesting.
- You are so enthusiastic about what you believe.
- That's a new thought.
- You may be right.
- You have studied this a lot.
- Incredible! I had not connected the dots this way.
- It's good to hear another side of the story.
- Are you comfortable with moving in this direction?

Using Precious Tools

Words require skilled implementation. They can be gifts of concern, caring, and encouragement—or weapons of rebuke, criticism, and rejection. They can with one phrase forgive and comfort, and with another sledgehammer ingratiating comments. Too often, when we are coping with a difficult person, our words become wedges that split open wounds and ax hope. When you must continue a working relationship with someone who twists your words, denigrates your efforts, or is nonresponsive, it pays to figure out how to keep your head on straight.

Covey suggests that positive communication listens to understand and then shares thoughts to work toward compromise.[5] With difficult people a fourth step must come into play: endurance. Listen. Share. Compromise. Endure. Communication may be as much about endurance and survival as conciliation and resolution. The goal is unity within diversity but, instead of expecting a hug and handshake, you hold on out of necessity—hang in there. The only thing that brings a screw out of the board it has been screwed into is a decision, a plan of action, and a lot of work.

> *Communication with a difficult person may be as much about endurance and survival as conciliation and resolution.*

Fortunately, most of the people with whom we work encourage and support us. It is a very few who cause us to feel mired in muck and swamped by chaos. The latter offer us great opportunities to develop self-control. Practice self-talk when your emotions are explosive. Try repeating these phrases as a mantra when your self-discipline is waning:

- The way I say something is as important as what I say.
- I am responsible for my words and acts.
- I must be sensitive to the need of every person to be heard and appreciated.
- I will be objective and detached in order to keep from becoming emotionally distraught.
- I will develop a plan of action based on the reality of what is possible.

- I will echo what I hear so misspoken or misinterpreted words can be reconsidered.
- I will correct misstatements tactfully but convincingly.

Watch the movie *Morning Glory* starring Harrison Ford, Rachel McAdams, and Diane Keaton if you are struggling with a co-worker who is noncompliant. In the movie, a young, compulsive executive director of a morning news program is fraught with staff problems. She works with impossible egomaniacs and a blunt, in-your-face supervisor whose remarks squelch self-esteem and hope. You will appreciate her emotions: the discouragement, embarrassment, and over-the-top "control" efforts. The movie is a comedy that, unfortunately, mimics real life. Dealing with irregular people is an everyday problem in the work world that requires tremendous effort and flexibility. At the end of the movie, the persevering program director, through her positive and sometimes confrontational actions, has turned an almost-impossible situation into a successful news program. You can do the same!

Be careful when giving advice. Fools won't heed it; wise men don't need it.

I am sure you have found that many difficult people have superb, creative, and needed talents and skills. They are not lacking in every department. The advice of Dr. Ronald Hamby on Alzheimer's becomes more relevant, when trying to get through to people who don't want to listen, than the platitudes in how-to books on communication: "Stop trying to reason with someone who is unable (or unwilling) to understand, and do what you must to protect and care for the individual (or at work, to protect and care for the business)."[6]

The question is not *if* but rather *when* you will have the opportunity to turn gruffness, self-focus, hostility, or any other alienating trait into cooperation. It might be helpful to consider this popular adage: be careful when giving advice. Fools won't heed it; wise men don't need it. But, oh, how grateful I have been at some of the crossroads in my life when a gentle soul reached out with a simple, kind suggestion, offered for my consideration, but also as a bit of wisdom gleaned from experience.

Insights

- Communication with most people is an art, but with difficult people it is an understanding that regardless of what you say, your words may be misinterpreted.
- Screwed-up people may misinterpret your words but read your body language clearly.
- The sandwich approach often opens deaf ears to the self-benefit of change.
- Words combined with kind acts may break through the communication barrier.
- Be careful when giving advice. Fools won't heed it; wise men don't need it.

Questions

1. Have you ever used the sandwich approach when you needed to be heard?
2. How good are you at reading body language, the thoughts behind the words?
3. Do you have a story of how humor turned a situation around?
4. What is the difference between humor that breaks down barriers and humor that cuts?
5. Can praise backfire on you? Why?
6. How do you keep echoing their words from becoming irritating to the listener?

18

Are You as Wise as a Donkey?

No amount of prejudice can affect how you feel about yourself unless you accept the judgment of others as truth.

A farmer's donkey fell into a deep pit. The animal bawled piteously for hours as his master tried to free his loyal beast of burden. Finally, the master wiped his brow and shrugged, thinking, *The animal is old. My back is tired. What shall I do?* He left the piteous animal to consult with his neighbors, who after assessing the seemingly hopeless situation, said, "Your donkey is old. His best years are behind him. Let's cover him with dirt and we will go on our way."

At first, the donkey brayed loudly with each clod of dirt that struck his back. How unfair! After all he had done through the years to help his master, now the farmer was covering him with dirt to die. He cried in dismay. Then all became quiet. The crowd

195

shoveling the dirt felt sad, for the donkey must be at the end, but what else could they do? They kept shoveling quietly. Finally, the master and his neighbors looked over the pit's edge. To their astonishment the donkey was alive and well. The donkey was old, but he was no fool. As the dirt had fallen upon his back he shook, stomped, and stepped higher toward the pit's lip. As the crowd looked on, the aged, used-up donkey sauntered up over the edge of the pit and happily trotted off!

Like the donkey, we will have times at work when we feel we are in a pit, being hit by prejudice shoveled because of our gender, age, nationality, disability, education, economic level, religion, political belief, personal characteristics, or whatever else offers others an excuse to pass over, downsize, overwork, criticize, or undervalue us. Bias in balance serves as a guide. Out-of-balance bias disrespects all contrary beliefs, stifles, labels, isolates, and is unjust. The farmer's bias that his donkey's age made the animal less valuable was grounded in some truth, but it failed to take into account that age brings experience and experience grows wisdom. The donkey was judged on an extraneous characteristic.

"I know how that donkey felt," my friend Martin commented. "I work in an office with a woman who just doesn't like me. She makes me want to bawl. If someone says something nice about me, she counters with a cutting remark. It got so bad that I went to her office and asked if I had done something to offend her. She just muttered."

Like Martin, you know bias when you feel it. Bias can be masked but it is impossible to completely hide. Bias affects employees in a myriad of ways: lower pay for the same job with equivalent qualifications, promotion denials, harassment, token employment for diversity's sake, reverse discrimination. Perhaps bias also shows in less tangible ways: your ideas are dismissed as insignificant because you are not part of the inner circle, the real meeting takes place after the official meeting when those who wield the power meet for a golf game or a beer, your team meets for lunch without inviting you, or you are asked to do things you feel are wrong.

There are a few simple truths about prejudice:

1. Bias is a natural response encoded through upbringing and experience.
2. Bias can be masked, but is impossible to completely hide.
3. Bias is felt and read in facial expressions, innuendo, and a sense of unfairness.
4. Bias drives us to anger, to quitting jobs, and to legal avenues.
5. Bias hurts both the prejudiced and the targets of prejudice.
6. Bias can be changed.
7. Bias belongs to the person who believes it.
8. Bias has power because it affects you and influences how others perceive you.
9. Bias has power to make you a victim if you allow it to define you.

Like all animals, we are stamped with beliefs that guide our thoughts and actions. Austrian naturalist Konrad Lorenz (1903–89) studied geese, chicks, and ducks. He found that there are critical periods in life where exposure imprints a learning (in humans, a belief) that is difficult, often impossible, to change. Birds coming out of their eggs follow and bond to the first moving object they encounter: a human, another type of bird, a dog, or even inanimate objects such as a ball. That object becomes the bird's parent. For example, a duckling raised by chickens will believe himself to be a chicken, and thereafter ignore other ducks, socialize with fellow chickens, and peck at the ground.[1]

197

Just because someone thinks we belong in the pit does not make it so.

Unlike animals, we can unlearn our biases if we discover them to be harmful or invalid. The startled farmer changed his prejudice toward his donkey when he saw the donkey's clever escape. We must be as wise as the donkey to figure out how to circumvent prejudice that threatens to limit our opportunities or drive us to do things we believe are wrong. Just because someone thinks we belong in the pit does not make it so.

Making Great Strides

It is obvious that as a country we have made tremendous strides toward equality in many work areas. A woman in the '60s was encouraged to be a nurse, secretary, or teacher. Hanna Rosin, in an essay titled "The End of Men," writes that today women make up the majority of the workforce in the United States.

> Women dominate today's colleges and professional schools—for every two men who will receive a B.A. this year, three women will do the same. Of the 15 job categories projected to grow the most in the next decade in the U.S., all but two are occupied primarily by women. . . . Men dominate just two of the 15 job categories projected to grow the most over the next decade: janitor and computer engineer.[2]

Still, gender bias is impossible to completely eliminate. If women are now as respected in the workplace as men, it would seem both men and women should be supportive of their sisters in power positions. "Not so!" says a Kentucky high school principal. "I feel tremendous pressure to outdo the male principals in my district to prove I am not just the token appointment, but it's like walking a tightrope: come on too strong and you are a target, too quiet and you are a mouse. I cope with a mostly female staff of teachers who seem intent on bringing me down. Maybe it feels easier to cozy up to a male than to justify requests to another woman."

Prejudice is hard to prove. Was this principal defensive because of her own bias, or was she dealing with the reality affirmed by research that a woman must outperform a man to be considered his equal? Could she turn the situation around by leadership that was up-front and open to suggestions from her staff? Would being vulnerable to other views move her staff from perceiving her as a dragon lady to a valued leader, or would it merely make her appear weak?

How Do We Handle Bias?

It's no fun to be the butt of someone's prejudice. Yet all of us will face prejudice, as surely as it is true that all of us have prejudice. We just are not necessarily prejudiced about the same things. A man in a board meeting of a charitable organization stated, "No one who grew up with plenty of money can possibly understand the needs of the poor. The rich are all prejudiced." The chairman, a man of great wealth, asked if he, in trying to make his point, had overstated the problem. "All?" he asked. The man nodded, "Absolutely, all!" Arguing would have won no points for either. Both did agree that there was much that could be learned about the needs of others, regardless of whether they had wealth or lived in poverty.

Bias can be masked and hard to prove but is impossible to completely hide.

Knowing what you believe and what you are willing to stand up for is crucial. Esmeralda Flores, who is from Honduras, works

199

on a cleaning team with Mexican co-workers. They locked her out of the dining hall at break time because she wasn't Mexican. I asked her how she dealt with the problem: "I just said, okay, and went on. If they want to act like that it is their problem, not mine." She chose to ignore the issue because it was not worth the fight. However, when a co-worker asked Esmeralda to overlook her stealing from the company because they were "sisters," Esmeralda chose to report the theft. "I did not get in a tizzy over their immature actions of locking me out of the break room, but I could not look the other way when their actions were illegal."

Some points are valid to discuss; some simply create walls.

It isn't easy to stand up for what you believe if those beliefs affect others negatively. No one likes snitches, tattletales, or someone whose actions make them look bad. Even government becomes involved to protect those who come forward with information of company wrongs. Does that stop the retaliation? Not if you talk with Dr. Jeffrey Wigand, former vice president of research and development at Philip Morris, a tobacco company. He left Philip Morris after the company demanded arsenic be added to the tobacco. He then cooperated with the Department of Justice case that alleged the cigarette industry purposely and fraudulently misled the public about the risks and dangers of cigarette smoking. What was the cost to him? His job, home, family, and friendships.

With all the rules and regulations in place now, overt discrimination is much less a factor in the workplace: only 15 percent experience it, according to the 2011 Gallup Poll.[3] Are we to believe that? Maybe it is so with the bigger issues, where companies must extend the same employment opportunities and enforce the same policies for each employee. Preferential treatment is not allowed. But interpersonal relationships in the office or factory are hard to legislate. A salesman complained that his peer group labeled him a religious nut because he chose to stay in less expensive hotels and eat frugally on business trips. "It's not fair to stick the company for expenses I would not spend if I were traveling on my own," he said. "I hate to be labeled a 'fanatic,' but I believe in doing to others what I would want them to do to me."

We live in a society that wants everyone to be politically correct. The press burned Dr. Larry Summers, the president of Harvard College, who was fired after publicly stating that women are genetically less capable in the sciences than men. He left Harvard, disgraced, for a job in Washington, DC, where you can be sure he will be coached in being more politic. Comedian Michael Richards (Kramer in *Seinfeld*) was riddled by media buckshot after using the "N word." His career in jeopardy, Richards became the poster child for everyone to watch not only their actions, but also the words they throw around. Not a bad idea, but no amount of media and societal policing about every misstatement or act will eradicate prejudice from the workforce.

> *Figuring out how to handle bias is easier if you know what you believe, but that doesn't make it easy.*

Removing the Chip on the Shoulder

Still, the way we handle prejudice can turn the tables for us, just as it did for the donkey who proved his shrewdness by using the dirt to climb up and out. Grace tears down the walls built by prejudice. I was impressed by the power of nonconfrontational assertion as I talked with a husband-wife entrepreneur team returning from a trip to investigate a franchise possibility. The husband handled the engineering aspects of their business development; the wife was the impetus behind investment and risk. The two had been ushered into the company's presidential suite to be greeted by the CEO, who put his arm around the wife and said, "Honey, I'm sure you would like to go with my assistant and have something to drink while we men do business."

Prejudice is much easier to overcome with a handshake than with a pie in the face.

That demeaning remark is enough to make most women cringe. I asked this business-woman how it made her feel. She just laughed. "I'm used to it. They figure out who makes the investment decisions when the discussions begin, but until then I can count on being considered a lesser figure in the deals because I wear a skirt."

Going around with a chip on your shoulder, looking for ways prejudice shows its face, isn't good for your psyche. It's better to laugh and go on about your business, even when it pops up. It is doubtful that CEO made such a miscall again after dealing with this woman—who with a smile signed on the line for franchises in five states. We learn prejudice. We also unlearn it, especially when the lesson comes with grace that allows a pie-in-the-face situation to end with a handshake instead of harsh words.

Gandhi and Martin Luther King Jr. argued that the only way to change inset prejudice was through non-force, expressing your beliefs without ill will or hostility. Argument or violence strengthens prejudice. I agree: the best way to handle prejudice is carefully, quietly, and without rancor.

Deal with It

There are five ways to handle bias: (1) you can internalize it and simmer, (2) you can accept it as true and don a victim mentality, (3) you can ignore it, (4) you can address it without rancor and state your view as you try to find common ground upon which you can agree, or (5) you can seek outside help to deal with it. Simmering or allowing someone else's prejudice to make you a victim leaves you powerless.

Most people handle discrimination issues by spinning off their anger to a friend or co-worker who understands and sympathizes. But there are issues that require legal help. The Equal Employment Opportunity Commission (EEOC) was established in 1970 to handle such cases. Calm yourself if you consider that the discrimination against you justifies legal action. Gather supporting evidence of the discrimination, comparisons, and statistical data of the preferential treatment. Concrete facts can open doors for you as it did for women in the 1970s seeking to be allowed into the exclusive "good ol' boy" clubs where networking and mentoring opportunities gave an edge to their male cohorts.

The best way to handle prejudice is carefully, quietly, and without rancor.

If you find yourself in a situation that will affect your standing, defend what you bring to the table. Address issues that might bias others against you. For instance, if you are pushing the age limit, project yourself as flexible, cheerful, and skilled. Review the benefits of hands-on experience, commitment to a career, and a track record of success, stability, and realistic expectations. Joyce Lain Kennedy's *Résumés for Dummies* suggests you stress only the last fifteen years of experience for a managerial job, ten years for a technical job, and five years for a high-tech job. Consider talking about your skills rather than chronicling your work years. For certain, let it be known you are computer literate.

Workshops such as those conducted by Barbara Annis encourage transforming the workplace by acknowledging the differences and biases between genders, races, ages, or any other area of prejudice.

Trying to act as if differences do not exist is like putting your head in the sand. She argues that focusing on the strengths your differences bring to the table allows you to debate out loud so that everyone feels a part of the team, as opposed to harboring and simmering.

Prejudice is the other person's blindness, not the truth of who you are.

Open discussion offers the opportunity to understand each other and often leads to small changes that bring strong cohesion to a group. Dwell on what you bring to the table, not what others may think of you.

If you were in a funk because someone rang your bell with their slight, gossip, or outright prejudice, I would advise you to talk your emotions down. Prejudice is the other person's blindness, not the truth of who you are. You can turn the strongest "I want to hit you" emotions around by simply saying to yourself, and to anyone who wants to add gasoline to your fire, how sorry you feel for the person who evaluates others on preconceived notions. You are in charge of you. Don't let someone else take that control away by their wrong acts. Exercise helps. Music soothes. Relaxing with someone you love refreshes and realigns your perspective. Put on your duck's back, and shed the negative like a duck sheds rain.

It helps to address the issue straight on at times, with no boxing gloves, no strike-backs, no slams:

- I don't feel that way.
- I think he/she has some great qualities.
- I certainly want to be supportive of company policy, just not this way.
- I feel you dislike me. I am sorry. I would hope we could work together amicably.
- Sorry, I feel uncomfortable doing what you are suggesting.

If you have grown up in a dog-eat-dog world it is going to be hard to look at people and see good qualities. It is far more likely you will growl and raise your defenses when hit by bias. On the other hand, if your home rivaled Ozzie and Harriet's in their eponymous 1950s television show, you will be hard-pressed to believe anyone could have a bad thought about you. Put aside naiveté. You are not locked into patterns that springboard off the past.

1. Recognize prejudice is the other guy's blindness, not the truth of who you are.
2. Feel sorrow for those who are prejudiced.
3. Keep on keeping on with your goals in mind.
4. Do what you should, regardless of what others do.
5. Have a duck's back, shedding the negative like duck feathers shed rain.
6. Let off some steam through exercise, music, hobbies, and camaraderie.
7. Talk with a confidant who will be an encourager and can help you evaluate tactics to stay balanced and focused on the positive role you play at work.
8. Relax with something or someone you love to refresh and realign your perspective.
9. Determine to handle prejudice with grace.

Remember the donkey? He was about to be sacked because his owner decided he was too old to warrant the effort of getting him out of the pit. How unfair was the farmer's and his neighbors' treatment as they threw dirt on his back! Not even a donkey likes being dissed. But this donkey knew bawling would get him nowhere. So the donkey studied his problem, then stepped aside and up until he was able to trot to freedom.

You aren't a donkey, but if you are reading this book you could be in a pit of your own. This is a good time to act like the donkey: stand up, shake off the crud, ignore the prejudice, and trot on.

Insights

- Bias can be masked and hard to prove, but is impossible to completely hide.
- Just because someone thinks we belong in the pit does not make it so.
- Figuring out how to handle bias is easier if you know what you believe.
- The best way to handle prejudice is carefully, quietly, and without rancor.
- Prejudice is much easier to overcome with a handshake than a pie in the face.
- Bawling gets you nowhere.
- Dwell on what you bring to the table, not what another may think of you.

Questions

1. Have you ever confronted prejudice?
2. Did you address the bias straight on or try to skirt it, hoping it would go away?
3. When you encounter prejudice, what tactics best counter it?
4. What is helpful encouragement for someone hit by prejudice?
5. Are there simple statements you could use to let others know you do not agree with a prejudice but will not start war games?

19

The Tug-of-War

When everything is coming your way, you are in the
wrong lane.

A recent study of more than fifty thousand employees from a
variety of manufacturing and service organizations found
that two out of five employees and four out of five professionals are
dissatisfied with the balance between their work and their personal
lives. This lack of balance "is due to long work hours, changing
demographics, more time in the car or office, the deterioration of
boundaries between work and home, and increased work pressure,"
says the study's author Bruce Katcher.[1]

Balance between home and work life is a moving target. Some
days, some years, you find your career demands require an inor-
dinate amount of time and energy. The right balance when you
are single will be different than when you marry or have children.
Balance will skew when the business is struggling to stay afloat

*B*alance between home and work life is a moving target that requires reflection and flexibility.

or meet all its commitments, just as balance in your life outside of work will skew with parental care issues or relationship struggles. The balance will be different when you begin your career or a new job versus when you are nearing retirement. Balance requires reflection and flexibility.

The fragile balance between work and home life is a seesaw. What is right today is wrong tomorrow. But consider the consequences of a poor work-life balance:

- **Fatigue.** Being overly tired means you will be less productive in all areas of your life. Tensions with co-workers, customers, family, and friends will escalate.

- **Loss of time with loved ones and friends.** Important family events and milestones will be missed, relationships harmed, and friendships abandoned when your balance skews. In turn, those negatives affect work relationships, responses, and actions.

- **Increased expectations.** The scale tips when you do more. The more you do, the more you are expected to do.

- **Irritability.** You can't do it all. But if you try, you may succeed temporarily. Eventually there will be a price to pay: your relationships at work or home, or your health.

Finding Balance

Consider these tips for achieving better harmony between your work and the rest of your life. You won't be happy if you simply stew about the problems. That negative energy will spin off at work and at home. Take time to reflect on these suggestions, and then set your priorities to find ways to stop being blown helter-skelter!

1. You can change positions or jobs if balance is not possible.

Before you quit, know it is easier to find another position when you are in a job or at the very least have a workable plan.

You may be happier in another position within your company or in a different job or career. But before you quit, know it is easier to find another position when you are in a job. The Bureau of Labor and Statistics reports that by age fifty the average person in America will have had fourteen jobs and change careers three times.[2] In Africa I met an American whose previous career in the New York Stock Exchange was far afield from his very successful new venture: a hot air balloon flight company that flew over safari areas following the animal migrations. I was surprised by such a career shift. He explained, "I couldn't figure out how to make both home and career work until I was watching a television special on the hot air balloon festival in Arizona with my wife. We asked ourselves, 'Why not?' And just like that we started planning our move. It took time, but the planning brought excitement back into our lives and made the problems at work far less consuming. Five years later we quit our jobs, moved countries, and set up shop."

2. Explore your options with your boss or your employees.

You may find needs at home and work have changed. Ask for help. Discuss options with your boss, partners, or co-workers. If your responsibilities at home are conflicting with your work schedule, consider saying, "I like my job and I think I am an asset. I picture myself staying with and growing with this company in the future. I'd like to talk about ways to make my work here as productive as possible as I struggle with some problems at home."

- State the problem. "I have a sick child, aging parents, and health problems."
- State the solution. "I feel I would be more productive and able to give my best if I could work twelve hours a day for four days a week. That would cut down on commute time, allowing me to pour myself into the job here and stay afloat at home."

Ellen Galinsky of the Families and Work Institute is a leading expert in the field of families and work. In an interview she emphasized how small businesses are helping to drive changes in the structure of work, offering employees more opportunities for workplace flexibility. For example, a 2010 study showed that 34 percent of companies let some employees change their starting and quitting times on a daily basis, and 45 percent let employees pay for childcare with pretax dollars. In this economic climate, when employers can't give raises, they may be willing to offer other benefits.[3]

Consider your needs and be open with your employer to see if there are options that can alleviate some of the stress. Discuss (without minutiae) the problem and solution with your co-workers only after your plans have been approved. You might be surprised how receptive others are to your plight. Balance is a problem for everyone, and if your co-workers or supervisors can help you through your difficult times, the possibility exists that you—or the company—will help them in turn. Also, your openness keeps co-workers from feeling your special treatment will force them into unwanted additional responsibilities that will throw their delicate balance out of kilter.

3. Get a grip.

You may have to deal with the reality that there is no good solution for the "issues" in your workplace. Get a grip, if job issues won't change and shifting to a new position or seeking a new job is not a possibility. A manager shared that his boss's decisions seem so illogical that at times he left the office to calm himself. "I felt he was killing the business, my job!" he said. "It was like watching the *Titanic* go down. I carried home crisis every night. Finally, I dealt with the reality that I would do what I could do, and not worry further about it. If my boss asked, I gave my opinion and then let it go. He owned the business; he could kill it. I would find another job."

4. Prioritize.

It isn't easy to figure out what is important, but you must try. Time is priceless. Be wise in how you give it away. Say no to superfluous activities that simply add to the complexity of your life. Perhaps you are doing the job that was originally allocated to three employees. Not good! It is merely a matter of time before something breaks down in such scenarios: your marriage, health, or patience. Focus on things that are important to you, and don't do the extraneous stuff. This is a discipline that doesn't come too naturally to most of us. Force yourself to edit yourself both personally and professionally.

> *Taking on everything threatens to keep you from doing well in anything.*

5. Don't sweat the small stuff.

This isn't as easy as it sounds. Technology is the small stuff that is supposed to make your life easier, not rule it. But it's hard to remember that when cell phones, faxes, texts, or emails demand return information immediately. Set aside time to respond when it does not interfere with more imperative duties. Taking on *everything* threatens to keep you from doing well in *anything*.

6. Establish boundaries.

Set limits and priorities for yourself. I was impressed by the wisdom and boldness of an executive assistant who upon answering her doorbell one evening found her boss with paperwork in hand. He asked her to type up his notes so he could review them first thing in the morning. I asked how she handled the situation. She replied, "I thanked him for bringing the notes to me, but told him I had plans for the evening and I would take the paper with me to work in the morning and put it ahead of my other agenda since it was critical. My boss is a workaholic. If I'd done the task that evening, I would have found him at my doorstep every night."

7. The goal is to work smarter, not harder.

Avoid procrastination. If it needs to be done, do it. Don't let it hang over you. Much of the stress and long hours employees work is due to their own inefficiency. An elementary principal who had superior skills in relating to his students and motivating his teachers lost his job because he didn't meet the paperwork deadlines required by his supervisors. Failure to meet the requirements of your position affects others, who are forced to be ogres to beat you into compliance or find someone else to pick up your slack.

8. Provide senior management role models.

Employees often take their cues from senior members of the organization. If they are workaholics, the rest of the organization will become workaholic. If they achieve balance in their lives, the rest of the organization will tend to do so as well. It will be hard for you to find balance in a company that expects your life to be work. You may be able to meet the challenge. The question is: Should you?

9. Slow down.

Don't lose the opportunities for positive relationships as you bury your head in your job duties, ignoring the people with whom and under whom you work. Speak to those you pass as you move through the business. Remember names. Recall special occasions or challenges with a comment. Schedule more time in team meetings and private conferences to allow face-to-face conversation. Never undervalue the importance of good vibes in your workplace.

A study of physician-patient relationships clearly shows that a physician who enters the patient's room, comments on something in the patient's life outside their health, touches the patient's shoulder or hand, and appears neither hurried nor harried will be perceived by the patient as doing a better job than a physician who stands at a distance coolly going over the medical facts, even though the former may spend less time with the patient. It takes only a moment to greet others, but those acts make a significant difference in company morale.

10. Take time for yourself.

All work and no play makes for nothing but trouble at work and at home. Why not take twenty minutes, a short spurt of time, to do something just for yourself? Maybe listen to music as you ride the commuter train instead of working on files. Perhaps jog or bicycle home, instead of driving. Maybe play with the dog, play catch with your child, sit down and enjoy a few minutes talking to someone you love, or visit with a friend before you start on your to-do list. Me-time eases tension.

Don't Say "I Can't!"

You may have only one choice if you stay with the company: keep up the pace. Most of us experience times it feels like the job is demanding far too much. But if the pressure is not going to ease in a reasonable time, consider your options and priorities. If your identity is your work, admit it to yourself and be willing to accept the price in your life outside of work.

If, however, you are trying to improve your balance, do not tell those affected by your work hours and tension that you can't do anything about it. Instead, explain the importance of keeping the pace and the reasons relief is not a current possibility. Discuss priorities as a family. Everyone may agree that the gains are worth the sacrifice. That relieves the pressure. But, if someone is filled with resentment, continue to discuss the issue. Affirm others for their willingness to sacrifice with you. Ultimately, the choice and its consequences are yours. Just be sure you can live with them.

Determining the time you give to home and to work is a priority choice. One attorney explained his compromise was tough at first. "I work like a madman for a month, then take my family for a short vacation or just spend a block of time at home. Now my family looks forward to the vacations and has grown to love their 'own' time, but that adjustment to their original idea of a nine-to-five workday didn't happen overnight. Same at work: it took time for the office to realize my family time, once set into the schedule, was sacred." The attorney agreed his schedule

> *Any road will take you someplace, but not necessarily where you want to go.*

214

worked because he refused to take company work with him when he was on *family* time, and worked whatever was needed when on *company* time.

There was a time when the boundaries between work and home were fairly clear. Today, however, work is likely to invade your personal life. Finding balance becomes a daily struggle with both work and home tugging you in opposite directions. You'll know when that balance is skewed because the stress will push your buttons. You could throw in the towel and cry "Game over, game over!" or choose to use your internal GPS system when tension rises: study your options, and recalculate.

We would all wish for a Goldilocks solution: work that is not too much nor too little, and not too hard nor too easy; work that gets us out of bed but gives us time to play. Wouldn't it be nice? But until that day comes, you may need to juggle. The challenge is to be intentional about your life choices, knowing balance requires effort! Remember, any road will take you someplace, but not necessarily where you want to go.

Insights

- Balance between home and work life is a moving target that requires reflection and flexibility.
- Taking on everything threatens to keep you from doing well in anything.
- Determining the time you give and how you give it at both home and work is a priority choice.
- Before you quit, know it is easier to find another position when you are in a job.
- Don't say, "I can't!"

- Any road will take you someplace, but not necessarily where you want to go.

Questions

1. Do you feel you have a good balance between home and work?
2. If not, what signs do you have that indicate your balance is skewed?
3. What can you do about it if it is out of balance?

20

Love It or Leave It

A Crossroads Decision

If you focus on what you left behind, you will never
see what lies ahead.

No one can answer for someone else whether staying the course
in a job is the best decision. Staying does not mean you are
stuck in the job. Leaving doesn't imply failure, a bad choice, or an
inability to cope with your co-workers. But staying while unhappy
and bitter or leaving while clinging to the injustices are both poor
course management.

For many of us the job we are in is not what we wanted to
do—and certainly not who we thought we were going to be when
we grew up. It is not what we thought our life was about. For these
people, quitting a job is an epiphany, a calling to follow a dream or
simply change direction. There is excitement and anticipation of

good things to come. But for most, quitting a job, that bird in the hand, is a difficult choice. It's like having an optional surgery. You wouldn't even consider it if there were no problem. Leaving implies your willingness to endure discomfort, inconvenience, emotional turmoil, and new stresses for the gain of a new beginning. Yet neither choosing to stay nor choosing to leave seems to affect the happiness of most of us. We stay, hoping things will change, or we leave only to find the same kind of problems that plagued us in one job are in the next, just dressed in different garb.

There are three courses to consider when determining whether to stay or to sever your ties at work. The first two, staying or leaving, are packaged with pluses and minuses that must be seriously evaluated. But the third course, straddling the fence, is always a poor choice. It not only messes with the heads of those with whom you work, it wraps you around the wrongs: what you are not getting, what they should do, who is unfair. This view is self-centered and self-absorbing. Frankly, it is a bad way to live life and is terrible for job satisfaction. No one wins if staying engages halfway, wishy-washy, lukewarm, or negative effort. No one wins if after leaving you dwell on the negatives from the previous job.

You may like the job, or just want the paycheck, but are stymied by the frustration of working with someone whose words or actions, like a fly's buzz, keeps you focused on irritating behavior. No job in the world is worth the effort needed to coexist with "acid reflux" people if your aspiration is merely money. But I imagine, if you have chosen a book like this, your goal is more than a paycheck. You want opportunities to make a difference, to use your talent and gifts, and to affirm that your life has purpose. You are also seeking something else: freedom. You don't feel free when you work beside someone who, regardless of your efforts, simply doesn't give a flip. Crossroads decisions are personal. They are the points in life that demand a move: left or right, up or down, in or out. Some are the result of a slow, almost inch-by-inch recognition that you can't stay as you are. Something has to change. Your dreams: Do you go for them, or hunker down to reality? Your messed-up relationships with co-workers: Do you hang on, or bail? Your dependent, energy-sucking team members: Do you keep dolling out fixes, or step back? Other decisions are a blast out of the blue, foisted on you by someone else. You pack up your pens and family photos as the resource director comments, "Sorry. It was a painful decision, but we have to downsize."

Know Your Limits

I met Douglas in a conference I was attending. I was surprised by his career story. Here was a man who was immensely successful, and had worked twenty years as head of production for a major, syndicated television game show, yet he described his host as A-plus: arrogant, antagonist, audacious, and asinine. He stated quite matter-of-factly, "Off-camera he was worse than a disaster. Every word from his mouth caused chaos. We walked on eggshells, waiting to be bombed by accusations and criticism. The job was a fruit-basket upset with employees constantly leaving." I was curious: Why did he stay? How did he stay?

Straddling the fence is a bad way to live life and is terrible for job satisfaction.

"The *why* is simple," Douglas said. "I liked my job and I knew I was needed. I was good, regardless of the host's maliciousness. The *how* was straightforward, but more complex: I knew he couldn't do his job without me being great at mine. I also knew he was the one who was off-the-wall. I didn't take his nasty remarks personally, even when they were aimed at me. In fact, I often addressed his cuts by saying, 'Must be having another bad day!' I knew my limits, and refused to allow him to cross them."

This man knew the keys to staying in a difficult situation:

- He liked his job tasks.
- He knew he was needed.
- He knew who was responsible for wrong acts.
- He knew his limits.
- He was unafraid to address the issues.

Still, there is a price to pay when life at work is a constant state of tension, even if, like Douglas, you seem able to handle the situation. Douglas quit his job with the production company to join a monastic order in New England that required a vow of silence. After his twenty-year stint with a difficult boss, it took him seven years before he felt like rejoining the work world outside of the protected environment of the monastery.

A word to the wise: many times a bad boss or employee can be outstayed, especially in large and multilevel companies, churches, schools, hospitals, and corporations. However, staying the course can be costly when the likelihood of change in a negative situation is as unlikely as it was in Douglas's company.

Why Quit?

You feel your time is past.

This is to be considered. On the other hand, you may place more weight on your shortcomings and failures than the staff who still recognize your value. One of my favorite Arab tales is of two clay vessels that serve a family.

Each morning the master of the house shouldered two empty clay jars to walk the long distance from his home to the stream for water. One vessel was new, beautiful, and sturdy while the other jar was cracked and old, scarred from many years of use. The master would fill each with water from the bubbling brook and traipse back home. When he arrived home, the cracked vessel was distressed. Water had spilled along the way, seeping through its cracks.

Know your limits, as well as why you stay, if you determine to not quit a difficult job.

"Master, master," cried the vessel, "you must put me away. I am old and cracked. My body is chipped. The water seeps through my seams. Though I would wish to serve you I am no longer able." The master looked with care at his old clay pot. He remembered its being formed, the years of heavy loads it carried without complaint, and his family laughing as they drank from its contents. "Precious vessel," the master said as he gently rubbed its side, "do you not know that because of you our pathway to the stream is filled with beauty? You water the flowers along the way as water trickles from your cracks."

You may feel like a worn-out vessel, feeling tired of controlling your emotions that seep out in response to the difficult people with whom you deal, feeling unappreciated, and wondering if your work makes any difference. Perhaps, however, others do appreciate your efforts, see you as a voice that calms the tension, and seek your wisdom and caring. It isn't age, cracks, or failures that makes us unable—it is our inability to recognize the flowers we are watering. Talk with the one using you to carry his water. He will either encourage you to stay, or affirm that it is time to seek other employment.

You may be a misfit for the company culture.

You really are an extra thumb. It could be the business's stage of development does not fit your gifts, as we discussed in chapter 7. Or you find the office culture offends your sensibilities. A college graduate in a part-time job quit because she was offended by the risqué jokes and foul language. Though she needed the money, the job wasn't worth the misery of trying to not appear prudish and still uphold her standards. Addressing the issue would have been ineffective.

Different people have different understandings.

Is it possible to alleviate difficult problems by talking through the issues with the appropriate person? A manufacturing company executive was in crisis due to a major customer's "got to have it now" orders that never met the production's cutoff deadlines. Smaller orders had to be set aside; additional employees were hired and pushed to handle the stack-up; customers were irritated by delays. Pushed to the wall by the extra expenses and grumbling employees, the company president called the offending customer

It isn't age, cracks, or failures that make us unable—it is our inability to recognize the flowers we are watering and the lessons we are learning.

and explained that deadlines were set to avoid the panic that happened when orders were rushed. The customer replied, "Oh, I have no problem with ordering earlier. I didn't think it mattered." The distress was unnecessary, and was easily resolved when the CEO was up-front about the problem. Quite often the same is true of other issues at work: one side is in distress, the other is unaware of the chaos—or doesn't care about it. Someone must be willing to address the problem.

Burnout from overload or repetition can push you to leave.

You may feel as if quitting is the only way to get back in balance. However, a sabbatical or several-week break, or even a change in position, might alleviate the feeling of burnout. It takes energy, enthusiasm, and time away from the office to be creative in the office. Check your options; leaving may not be the only possibility to ease your tension.

Naiveté may be part of the problem.

If your discouragement is the result of not getting along with someone at work, it may be easy to eliminate by simply refusing to allow his or her actions to get under your skin. You aren't at work to win friends and influence people, though that may be the result if you handle *you* wisely. Address the issues face-to-face with the individual, or with whomever is responsible for overseeing such problems. Studies are conclusive: when you let something go on longer than it should, whether it's a relationship struggle, a wrong job decision, or accommodating a customer who refuses to follow the guidelines, you do more harm than good. Many gnat issues become gargantuan because we center on the irritation instead of the resolution.

Many issues at work spiral out of control because people have different understandings.

An audiologist was distressed to find that the assistant to the supervisor was altering her emailed reports. She met with the co-worker and addressed the issue, only to be countered by denials of wrongdoing. The same person altered the next report too. This time, however, the audiologist presented the hard copy of the original report to her supervisor, who then took steps to ensure the unauthorized changes would not happen again. The audiologist was keen and shrewd. She was up-front about the issue with the assistant, and then when the actions continued she went straight to the supervisor with evidence in hand.

Many gnat issues become gargantuan because we center on the irritation instead of the resolution.

She didn't grovel or plead with the assistant, naively thinking, *Surely she didn't intend to be so malicious.* Nor did she allow the wrong to continue unabated.

Expecting everything at work to be rosy is naive. Even roses have thorns. Yet when quitting is the course you choose, make certain you can live without your income, even temporarily. If possible, wait until you have a new job lined up to quit. Revise your résumé, look for job openings, and prepare for job interviews. Let your network contacts know your job situation has changed, but exercise caution here. If you have not decided to leave for certain, or when you will leave, you should not broadcast your plans. During the interim, do whatever you can to improve your situation as opposed to simply staggering through each day under the weight of issues that will seem heavier with each passing day.

Addressing the Problems

It is an even more difficult choice to leave a job in the current down economy, which shows the loss of eight million jobs with an unemployment rate rising to a twenty-six-year high of 10.1 percent. The number of people quitting their jobs has plummeted to the lowest number the government has recorded since 2000.[1] Seriously consider whether resolving your workplace issues might affect your decision to stay or leave your current job.

You might also want to ask yourself these true or false questions before you make your final decision of whether to stay or leave your job. If most of your answers are "false," perhaps you may resolve your discontent by tackling the specific issue of discord at work. Likewise, many "true" answers may help you determine the need to investigate other job or career options.

True or false:

1. You feel overqualified for the job.
2. The feeling of burnout and stress are making you physically sick.
3. You are being asked to do things that are unethical or illegal.
4. Your job performance reviews are unsatisfactory.
5. Home responsibilities are causing you to feel stressed by the job demands.
6. You can afford to quit.
7. You are bored.
8. You are having a problem getting along with co-workers or a boss.
9. You feel the need for a career change.
10. You are being passed over for promotions.
11. You feel sidelined even though your experience level should make you a valuable asset.
12. Your commute to work is too long.
13. A change in policies is unacceptable to you.
14. You do not like the company's direction.
15. You received an offer for a better job.

Deciding to Stay or Leave Has One Requirement: Quitting

One of football's great tragedies happened at the Mini Dome, on October 26, 1985. During the first quarter of a game between The Citadel and East Tennessee State University, nineteen-year-old

Citadel linebacker Marc Buoniconti was "speared" by Herman Jacobs, ETSU's star tailback. Buoniconti rolled over, his neck dislocated and his spine severed at the third and fourth cervical vertebrae.

While any injury of this magnitude would be terrible news, the name *Buoniconti* in football was sure to attract national media attention. Nick Buoniconti, Marc's father, had a stellar professional football career as linebacker with the Miami Dolphins. During his years there, the team advanced to three consecutive Super Bowl appearances. Sports fans felt Marc had all the makings of another sports hero.

That fateful night Marc began a journey that has been replete with struggles, failures, and successes. He survived the initial medical crisis and pain because he did not quit and did not give up. Then, when his condition stabilized, he won his life back because he did quit. He quit looking back, and quit focusing on what was gone. He determined to find a way to turn his loss into gain. Today Marc, a quadriplegic for more than twenty-five years, is actively involved in and provides the face of a project for which his family and the business community of Miami have joined hands, the Miami Project to Care for Paralysis. The program boasts a staff of 250 people and a $40 million research center. So far, it has raised $300 million for spinal injury research to find a cure for paralysis caused by spinal cord injuries. It currently has a research project involving Schwann cell transplants on human subjects, a regime that has already been successful in restoring 70 percent of spinal cord function in lab animals.[2]

> *Settle your commitment one way or another, knowing that either path exacts a price.*

Crossroads, whether a health issue, a relationship problem, or related to your job, demand Marc Buoniconti–style determination. No focus on loss, on wrongs, or on injustice. No straddling the fence. Stay or leave, but do so committed to winning. How? Settle your commitment one way or another, knowing that either path exacts a price. Commitment is a decision; it is also a process that gives you back your life. Being passive wraps you in a victim mantle. The indispensable first step to getting the things you want out of any career or job is this: decide what you want.

Upon leaving, express excitement and gratitude for the relationships and job experience.

If you decide quitting the job is best:

1. Resign from your job with dignity. Know your company's resignation policy. The minute you say "I quit," some companies will usher you out the door; others will hope for leeway time to secure someone to fill your role. Tell your boss first, not a co-worker. You do not want the gossip line to transmit your plans before the higher-ups are aware of your intentions.

2. Leave your job peacefully. You don't need to tell co-workers the negative reasons you are leaving. Be assured, most have a good idea of the drivers that cause those working with them to quit. Badmouthing and being spiteful will only boomerang back to slam you. Instead, express excitement and gratitude for the relationships and the job experience. No matter how wonderful or terrible it might have been, you gleaned tremendous lessons of what (or what not) to do.

A physician let go from his position at a major hospital because of conflict with the hospital CEO sought another job. His qualifications and work experience put him ahead of other candidates. Yet he didn't get the new position because during the interview process his anger and resentment toward the hospital management were expressed loudly and repeatedly. The office seeking to hire a physician understood his dismay and even felt aligned with his appraisal of the injustice. Still, they did not want to add someone to their staff who would tip the fragile balance their professionals had with the same hospital group. Be careful. No matter how right you may be in feeling your previous employer was the devil incarnate, it is grace in handling such challenges that wins every time.

3. **Protect your health insurance coverage.** When you quit your job, your employer will stop paying for your group health insurance. Two laws help prevent your being left without coverage: COBRA and HIPPA. COBRA lets you continue coverage while HIPPA lets you get new insurance, either on your own or through your spouse's employer, without having to worry about pre-existing conditions or enrollment periods. Be careful, for even if you move immediately to a new job there may be a waiting period imposed by a new employer.

> *Decide what you want. Commitment is a decision; it is also a process that gives you back your life.*

4. **Remember to ask for future recommendations.** Your next job is probably going to want a recommendation from your current one. Of course, if you are leaving on bad terms this may be a moot point. But if you are able to leave on amicable terms, a good recommendation from a former boss is worth a lot of weight.

5. **Don't steal anything or damage something to get even.** The "they deserve a kick in the pocketbook" attitude probably won't break the company bank, but it certainly will put you on bad footing for future opportunities. Plus, like pulling out a chair from under someone as a joke, such action highlights your immaturity.

Giving In to the Pressure

There are days we all may dream of quitting our jobs in a spectacular fashion, but Steven Slater actually did it! Steven Slater, a Jet Blue flight attendant, is now famous for quitting his job in one of the most outrageous ways imaginable: screaming at passengers and jumping down an emergency slide. Many applaud his action that said clearly, "Take this job and shove it!" Was the momentary crash-and-burn worth it? Maybe not! Slater was arrested for reckless endangerment and now, dealing with the reality of unemployment, wants his job back.

People wisecracked about their perfect version of leaving a job in a class I was conducting. Some told their real stories of quitting. Janie told us, "I was yelled at all week, asked to bill clients for hours that were inflated, and received email pornography from co-workers. I thought, to heck with it! I walked out. No notice, no backup plan, a mini–Steven Slater checkout." Michael offered his less flamboyant experience. "After being slapped by my kitchen manager, I was determined to find another job. When I did, I gave a two-week resignation notice. It was beneath me to fight with a nutcase."

Movies come up with creative and dramatic ways to handle the problems at work. Remember the three secretary-assistants in the Dolly Parton movie *Nine to Five* who kidnapped their boss and held him hostage until he agreed to their demands? In real life I don't recommend you kidnap the problem in your office, walk out like Janie, or leave with the drama of Steven Slater. But, if taking all into consideration, it is time to go, I do agree with Michael that there is a best way to go about quitting, regardless of how bad your worst day on the job gets: quietly, and with a plan in hand!

Insights

- Sitting on the fence is a bad way to live life and terrible for job satisfaction.
- A job offers more than employment. It is an opportunity to grow up and a chance to make a difference.

229

- Know your limits as well as why you stay if you determine not to quit a difficult job.

- It's tough to be satisfied if your center of concern at work is "what's in it for me."

- Naiveté has no place if you choose to quit a job.

- Decide what you want.

- Express excitement and gratitude for the relationships and job experience if you quit.

- Commitment is a decision; it is also a process that gives you back your life.

Questions

1. Do you need a new job or a new career?
2. Are you going to find the same kind of problems in the next job as you have in your current one?
3. Have you considered the practical issues of a job change: insurance, income, commute time, and so forth?
4. Have you planned your exit strategy, deciding the best way to tell fellow employees, to ask for recommendations, and to express thanks?
5. What will you do to alleviate some of the tension in your job if you stay?
6. Have you considered carefully all the options: sabbatical, vacation, changing positions, and so forth?

21

Handicapped, but Not Crippled

Attitude is a little thing that makes a big difference.

Jon Spoelstra, in his book *Marketing Outrageously Redux*, tells of an edict by Mao during the Cultural Revolution. Every man, woman, and child of the billion people living in China was to catch and kill one hundred flies. That would be one hundred billion flies caught and killed.[1] Did it rid the country of flies? Of course not! Screwed-up people and flies always survive. You can't get rid of them! But you can successfully work with them and come to appreciate what they bring to the company table.

Your work family, just like your personal family, isn't anybody's fault. They just are who they are. Like it or not, that presents you the opportunity to care "in spite of." Such action speaks volumes not only to the curmudgeon whose convoluted behavior stirs your emotions, but also to others who recognize your internal control. Your positive response to negatives is not only a lighthouse for others to follow, but also for the difficult person who recognizes there is something different about your reactions to him.

Handicapped, but Not Crippled

Opportunity comes in all kinds of packages. Dick Hoyt anguished when the doctor said, "Your son was strangled by the umbilical cord during birth. For your sake, consider putting him in an institution. He'll be a vegetable the rest of his life." He and his wife Judy didn't—and their son Rick isn't. As he grew they did what they could, even took him to Tufts University to see if the engineering department could invent something to help their son communicate. "No way! There is nothing going on in his brain," they were told. They didn't give up. They knew Rick listened, laughed at jokes, and responded appropriately to their words. They tried one thing after another, finally rigging up a computer to equip their mute quadriplegic son to peck out his thoughts, which he did in volumes.

A screwed-up person offers you the opportunity to care "in spite of."

Like the Hoyts, you know it is hard work figuring out what can help in difficult situations! This was no easy time for their family, nor is it easy for you to deal with people who cause you anguish. Dick said he became a "porker," with too much to do at work, causing him to come home too tired to exercise. A charity run organized for a school friend became the key that began to turn the world around for the Hoyt family. Rick typed, "Dad, I want to do the run!" A run seemed a daunting task to Dick, but he was determined to try.

Today, Dick Hoyt has pushed and pulled his 110-pound disabled son in ninety-five marathons. He has completed six Iron Man triathlons, pushing Rick twenty-six miles for the run, pulling him 2.4

miles for the swim, and then biking 112 miles with Rick in a seat on the handlebars. Dick has pulled his son cross-country skiing, taken him on his back mountain climbing, and once even hauled him across the country on a bike. At ages sixty-six and forty-four, Dick and Rick finished their twenty-fifth Boston Marathon, in 5,083rd place out of more than 20,000 starters. Their best time? Two hours, forty minutes, in 1992—only thirty-five minutes off the world record, which, in case you don't keep track of these things, happens to be held by a guy who was not pushing another man in a wheelchair at the time.[2]

Rick told his dad after a race, "You know Dad, when we are racing, I don't feel disabled anymore."

Dick agreed. "We all were better when we started focusing on what we could do, rather than centering on all Rick couldn't do." Dick and Judy couldn't prevent their son's handicap, but their actions did prevent his feeling *crippled*. It also probably saved Dick's life. After he had a mild heart attack during a race, his doctor told him that if he hadn't been in such great shape, he probably would have died fifteen years ago.

Dealing with screwed-up people is like running a marathon. It's taxing. It's easy to fall into the "porker" mentality—stymied, overwhelmed, and unable to figure a way out. At the same time, you find an inner strength if you refuse to be cocooned by the anxiety and tension that spin off interactions with a wearisome co-worker. Your actions that are nonconfrontational offer the person an opportunity to grow by your example, even as they encourage others struggling with a "handicapped" team member.

You will change. There is empowerment in being able to control the way you act within difficult relationships. You may not be able to prevent or change someone from being emotionally handicapped any more than Dick Hoyt could have prevented his son's handicap.

The good news is that like he gave Dick, God may be giving you the opportunity to keep a person from being a cripple.

Attitude, the Overriding Powerhouse

I find it helpful to use simple adages or stories, such as those I have written in this book, to program into my mind-set a way to control my emotions when I feel myself engaging in negatives. These simple thoughts rally my weakening spirit. I am able to disengage, rather than emotionally circling the drain. I can address off-base actions up-front, instead of internalizing them. Staying objective keeps me from powdering irregular acts into dust that fills my inner being and messes with my head. Remember: we can steer in any direction we choose with the right mind-set.

> You may not be able to prevent or change someone from being emotionally handicapped, but God may be giving you the opportunity to keep a person from being a cripple.

Your happiness and sense of satisfaction are all about you: your attitude and your choices. That isn't to say you won't experience plenty to challenge even the most positive mind-set, but if you do what every thriver (not survivor) does, you will be able to wade through the depths of unexpected, crashing waters without drowning in self-pity, anger, or overwhelming hurt. All thrivers embed stories and phrases in their minds.

Doing Your Best in the Everyday Ordinary

Those who become beacons of light at work are those not concerned with what the other guy does; they are concerned with being their very best in the "everyday ordinary." That is what made

Capt. Chesley "Sully" Sullenberger a hero, not just his amazing feat of landing a crippled US Airways jet in the Hudson River without the loss of a single life, which we all marvel at and decry as almost miraculous. In Sully's bestselling book *Highest Duty*, he describes his life as a simple commitment to do his best in the ordinary virtues in his career and his family. In doing so he embraced what we think of as quintessential American values: caring, doing right, and being responsible.

You will determine to do your best in the everyday ordinary if you are to be a cut above the rest.

Sully joined hands with people he wouldn't choose to be his best friends but who were his work partners. He knew, as you will find, that there is no such thing as perfection in the workplace, if for no other reason than that everyone has up and down days, days there are a million things to do on top of the job tasks: shopping, handling kid stuff, meeting a bevy of needs. There are times it is hard to plow into the chores at work. But, like Sully, if you are to feel good, you must give your best. Self-satisfaction doesn't flow from just getting by.

Sully's comments reminded me of a young woman who, after a visit with her counselor, declared, "The counselor said I gave too much in my marriage. I guarantee I'll never give so much again." What poor advice! In defense of the counselor, I imagine he was trying to get across the point that in her relationship she had become a doormat, lying down in deference to another's ideas and running on a treadmill to please. That is unhealthy at home or at work. Marriage is a partnership, a working-together relationship. The same is true at work. You are hired because you have something to contribute. What you do, your commitment to your job task and to those whose lives you touch, gives you the same opportunity as Sully or Lincoln: the chance to make a difference.

Coping with the Flies

Life rarely turns out to be what you thought it was going to be. You believe your boss should be your mentor; perhaps God put you in her life to be *her* mentor. You feel your co-workers darken the workplace; bring sunshine to the job. Someone above must believe that you are the precise person to change lives in this particular place where you spend half your day.

Remember, heroes aren't those who lived, worked, or died in perfect situations. *They are those who realize that happiness is not the result of having what we like, but rather liking what we have.* They are the ones who know it is not what you do when you get knocked down that matters; it is what you do when you get back up. It's recognizing that much of job satisfaction comes from the relationships you develop as you work toward building a successful business.

> *Happiness is not the result of having what we like, but rather liking what we have.*

Mao couldn't rid his country of flies. You won't rid your workplace of people challenges. But perhaps, as you address your work problems, this poem by Mother Teresa can help you focus on what makes long-term differences for your personal sense of well-being and joy. The poem was written on the wall in Mother Teresa's home for children in Calcutta.

> People are often unreasonable, irrational, and self-centered.
>   Forgive them anyway.
> If you are kind, people may accuse you of selfish, ulterior
>   motives. Be kind anyway.
> If you are successful, you will win some unfaithful friends
>   and some genuine enemies. Succeed anyway.

If you are honest and sincere, people may deceive you. Be
honest and sincere anyway.

What you spend years creating, others could destroy overnight. Create anyway.

If you find serenity and happiness, some may be jealous. Be
happy anyway.

The good you do today will often be forgotten. Do good
anyway.

Give the best you have and it will never be enough. Give
your best anyway.

In the final analysis, it is between you and God. It was
never between you and them anyway.[3]

My hope is that this book has encouraged you to thoughtfully
consider your responsibility to be a positive influence at work. I
hope if you have not yet asked yourself why you are in this particular job with these particular people, you
will do so. Your job offers more than employment. It is an opportunity to grow up and a
chance to make a difference, not only in the
tasks of work, but by simple acts of kindness,
by example, and by caring for the people who
are part of your work family in spite of the
challenges. Easy? Of course not!

> *It is not what you do when you get knocked down that matters; it is what you do when you get back up!*

As you encounter people in your workplace who frustrate you to your core, I hope
you will use insights from *Working Successfully with Screwed-Up
People* as lifelines. You can be sure I will be wishing for you the
same as I would wish for a dog who encounters a skunk eating
from his food bowl: *patience and wisdom!*

Insights

- The more difficult a person is, the more opportunity you have to learn what not to do.
- Relatives in a work family, just as in your personal family, aren't anybody's fault.
- Happiness is not the result of having what we like, but rather liking what we have.
- Remember: we can steer in any direction we choose.

Questions

1. Do you have special ways to reset your thoughts when your focus is drawing you to the negative?
2. Why is it hard to recognize when your focus is on the negative track?
3. Is there someone handicapped at work that, through your actions, may not become a cripple?
4. Would focus on the phrase "this too shall pass" help you feel less helpless in a difficult situation at work? Why or why not?
5. How can you help someone stuck on the negative shift his or her focus?

22

Answering the Questions

Work issues are plentiful. We have addressed many of the roots and possible solutions throughout this book. These are just a few of the questions I have been asked through the years. You might identify with a question asked by another worker just like you, trying to find a way to survive while working with a screwed-up person.

You may want to ask your co-workers to make a list of such questions for discussion in a work session. You may be surprised by the wealth of understanding and tact gleaned by others who have dealt with difficult people in their work world.

1. What are the rules about office romances? A supervisor dating a subordinate is probably frowned upon, but what if they are in different departments? I have seen so many flings and outright flagrant affairs in our company. Sometimes it's fine but other times everyone is abuzz about the situation.

There are no "rules" unless you are in a company that has established them. Some offices discourage any kind of romantic involvement or family working within the same company because they are a distraction and make workers less efficient. If the romance is between a supervisor and a subordinate and it doesn't work out, it opens the door to accusations of sexual harassment and potential lawsuits.

Many a lifetime of love has started in the office where workers get to know each other, first as friends and then moving on to romance. Many more romances have died on the vine. So while the temptation may be there, what's *right* most often is to avoid them and what is *wrong* is to get involved in what at the very least is risky business.

2. I work in a small office with a smelly man. He literally stinks. I don't want to hurt his feelings but it is hard to work beside him every day. Surely he wonders why people avoid him. Should I say something?

The best person to handle this type of issue is a supervisor. He or she is responsible for handling problems that have the potential to fire up tension, as well as addressing issues that affect the work environment. The supervisor can do it discreetly, asking about health issues and cleanliness, and making suggestions that would be offensive coming from a co-worker. It is far more likely personal hygiene will be changed if a job is in jeopardy than if a cohort makes such a suggestion.

3. Can you say no when offered a new position or move by the company?

The word from those who know is "No!" That can be tough. The issue is priorities when faced with a critical decision that will affect your life and those in your family. "No" may be what you determine is best for your life. Negotiate, state clearly why you are not willing to accept the offer, and be willing to accept the consequences. Who knows? You may be respected for your position—or not! Sometimes only time will tell.

4. I feel like my boss is a hurricane when she gets in my face and starts a torrent of blame or criticism of my work. How do I handle a boss's unreasonable criticism when I need the job?

Carefully. Figure out if this behavior is her tactic for getting you to do what she wants or part of her power game. Listen attentively. If the torrent is getting to you, picture her as a storm blowing through. She blows, she leaves. Your skin is wash-and-wear, so go on about your work if the comments are off-base. If, however, the comments, though poorly delivered, are valid, accept the criticism as instructive.

5. What is the trait most needed to handle difficulties at work?

How about the top three traits: perseverance, adaptability, and forgiveness. By perseverance the snail reached the ark. By adaptability chameleons stay alive in changing environments. By forgiveness one lives with peace in the present, not bound by the past.

6. I've stayed the course in a job I can't stand with people who drive me crazy because I work with family. I am not a quitter. But when is it time to bow out and move on with my life?

It sounds to me like you think holding on and hanging in there are signs of strength. But there are times it takes much more strength to know when to let go. And even more to do it. Only you know the time. If the job has become work, you might think whether it is worth continuing on, even if you are in a family business!

7. I know a woman who is stealing from our company. She's been employed here for years, but times are hard at home right now. She's a decent person and I am sure as soon as things settle down in her life, she will try to pay back what she has taken. Should I tell my boss?

Your co-worker is stealing and you ask if you should tell? Embezzlement, theft—these are crimes and your knowledge makes you an accomplice. Immediately notify the proper authority at work. Let them make the call of whether she is a "decent" person and intends to pay back what she has taken.

8. I feel invisible at work. No one even knows I am here. People pass and never say hello. Do you have suggestions?

Absolutely. Say hello first. Smile when you see someone. Wish them a good day! You may be sitting there feeling invisible as they pass; they, in turn, might wonder if you know they are passing.

9. I am afraid of my co-worker. There is something wrong. Should I speak to someone about my fear?

Yes. Immediately. Tension, pressure, or mental concerns create unsafe issues in our workplaces. Your business is no more immune than any other. If you suspect something is wrong, speak to a person who has the power to check it out. If it proves to be an invalid feeling, you can relax. If the suspicion proves to be on target, you may have helped someone get the help they need.

10. My co-workers are so competitive it drives me bonkers. It seems a lot of jobs are that way. Can you suggest a career where the workers will not be constantly vying to be top dog?

Have you ever been to the supermarket when the cashier opens another checkout line? Competition begins at birth and ends at death. Eventually most people learn to temper their need to be the line leader, but it is usually a slow process. You could lead the way by being more laid-back and less reactive, opening the door for others to act the same. But, as for suggesting another job, I doubt you will find the people in another job different from your current co-workers.

11. I am a floor manager. Regardless of what I suggest, one of my cohorts always answers back with another possibility. I feel like

Mother Tyrant asserting my power when I come back with "This is the way it is to be done." What should I do?

Calm down. Your co-worker is an external thinker. She popcorns her thoughts into words. Acknowledge her suggestion as positive. "Thank you for the suggestion but I want to do it this way because . . ." Some people think to themselves; others think out loud. Her behavior is normal for external thinkers, and will be less irritating if you recognize the thought process. She might even suggest a better way. But, regardless, it is your call that sets the agenda. Knowing that, be kind enough to show a bit of respect for being offered another possibility.

12. I work in a job I don't particularly enjoy, especially when I have to deal with some of the crazies at work. Any suggestions?

Yes! Try imagining yourself without a job—and absolutely no hope of finding one!

13. One of my co-workers tells everything about her personal life, including the secrets of her bedroom forays. It is incredibly disturbing. Am I being too secretive to want to keep my personal life to myself?

Secretive, no! Smart, yes! Personal issues can negatively affect your job and career. Sharing escapades, either face-to-face or on Facebook, is a no-no to people seeking employment or wanting to hold on to their jobs. Why allow negative thoughts about your personal choices to affect the way your co-workers appraise your work?

14. I'm a clutter buff. I like my stuff around me but the office rules don't allow it! This is my space. Should I revolt against such nonsense rigidity?

Follow the rules if you signed on to the job. Why allow such a little concern to become a major, disruptive issue? Consider the work problems that abound. You may be swatting at a gnat while a rampaging elephant is romping somewhere in your office.

15. Everyone tells me my job will get easier as I get into it. But right now it's the pits. I'm ready to try something else. Is quitting wrong?

Quitting is not wrong; in fact, sometimes it is the right thing to do. But, if you are quitting because the job requires hard work, you might want to consider that diamonds are nothing more than chunks of coal that stuck to their jobs.

16. I consider my faith very important. Is it wrong to share my religious views in the workplace?

The best way to share your faith at work is to live out your faith. It speaks louder than words. No one wants to work with someone who is preaching, but it's a rare bird who doesn't appreciate someone who is slow to anger, caring, appreciative, responsible, forgiving, and believes there is good in everyone.

17. I had an emergency this morning at home, so I was late to work. The supervisor was angry I had not called so she could make arrangements for someone to take care of my duties. I knew I could handle things when I got to work, so why was she upset?

Because you were discourteous! A simple call would have alerted her to your problem and when to expect your arrival. Not knowing, she did not want to call in extra help, nor did she want to pick up the pieces or deal with the chaos from not having someone at your station. Like it or not, at work you are part of a team. A team is a lot like a hand: if the thumb doesn't cooperate, the fingers struggle.

18. My days at work drag by. I count the minutes until Friday at 5:00. How can I make the days less tedious?

Find a job you like with people you enjoy and you add five wonderful days to every week.

19. I have a great education, a gifted mind, and lots of ability. I don't understand why I am in a lackey position when I have so much more ability to do more challenging tasks.

The only job where you start at the top is digging a hole.

20. I finally figured out that working for somebody will make me feel like life is long, even if I die young. The problem is I don't have the foggiest idea how to start my own business. Do you have a suggestion?

There's no scarcity of opportunity to make a living at what you love. There is only a scarcity of resolve to make it happen. Ask yourself: What would I be happy doing even if I were not paid for it? That's where you start. Planning becomes exciting. You want others to enjoy what you make, the talent you share, or the help you offer. The people you employ or serve will be friends because they share your vision. Nothing offers more potential for success than doing something you enjoy so much you almost feel guilty getting a paycheck.

21. I want to retire early. I have the money, so why not?

Are you unhappy at work? If so, you have the opportunity to shift to a new career that fulfills your dream of something new. Successful retirement—one you enjoy long-term—requires a plan and gusto for serving, creating, and doing. Spend all your time on the golf course or in home-command mode, and you may cause chaos in your relationships—or worse, become fodder for growing daisies.

22. I'm no spring chicken. I've been out of the job market a long time. How am I supposed to handle a difficult boss who is younger than me?

Just like you would a difficult child. "Praise his achievements, ignore his tantrums, and resist the urge to sit him down and explain to him how his brain is not fully developed."[1]

245

23. I'm afraid if I try something new I will be criticized, so I stay in my "safe zone" and miss opportunities to advance. Why am I so afraid I will trip as I try to make it up the ladder of success?

Maybe you feel like an advancement is a huge mountain to climb and you will slip, affirming to your co-workers that you weren't up to the grade. Perhaps it will help you to know that nobody trips over mountains. It is the small pebble that causes you to stumble. Success builds upon itself so that the skills you need for the next part of your journey are being fine-tuned in this part of your job. I never heard of anyone stumbling on something while sitting down, but neither do they experience the exhilaration of new experiences and new vistas.

24. My co-workers keep food at their workstations. It's like a feeding trough around me. I can't stop thinking how unhealthy the snacks are, how difficult it is to lose weight once it becomes layered, and how unprofessional it makes our office. Have you advice as to how to talk to the snack-food crowd about this?

Yes. My advice is to stay out of this snake pit. No snake has more venom than one protecting its food source. I suspect you are thin and good for you! Maybe, if your office manager is content with the situation, your example of a clean area and healthy eating habits will encourage some of your team members to follow suit.

25. I blew it! My steam was spewing and my words volcanoed at one of my co-workers. The creep copied my work and passed it off as his own. He was wrong but I shot off a vocabulary that even I was shocked I knew—in front of the whole staff. I feel like crawling under a rock. What should I do?

Grow up! You blew it. Pull yourself together. Say you are sorry. Admit you were shocked by your own words. Everyone knows why you lost control, so don't try to justify it. More likely than not, an employee who accepts responsibility for his actions is let off the clothesline where he would dangle if he tries to excuse his behavior. Handle the repercussions as lessons and move on.

26. I always dreamed of working in a job where everyone gets along and works to make a difference in the world. Yuck. My dreams have turned to dust. I'm so discouraged! How do I turn my enthusiasm back on?

If your dreams have turned to dust, vacuum. Reality is far more exciting than dreams. It seems your job is filled with screwed-up people who give you a great opportunity. Be sunshine. Be light. Be enthusiasm. Nothing is more contagious. You may infect your whole work world with a new zest just by refusing to be dragged down by someone else's lack thereof! Hang in there!

27. I work with someone I detest. I see this person quite often in social situations. I feel so uncomfortable trying to act like a friend. How should I handle the situation?

Smile. Greet your co-worker pleasantly. Move on to talk with another person in the room. Working with someone does not obligate you to be best friends after work hours. Common decency, however, does demand courteous behavior. By the way, the more serious issue is that hanging on to loathing is like letting that person live rent free in your head.

28. Ouch! Another job downsized. I'm about to give up. Help!

Get up and get going. "Life is not about how fast you run or how high you climb but how well you bounce."[2]

Appendix 1

The Personality Zoo

Have fun with this overview of ten personality types and their traits. Envision that you work at a zoo. Each personality type is coupled with an animal that exemplifies its characteristics. What animals resemble you and the people with whom you work? Are those in your office zoo sly as foxes, stubborn as mules, lazy as koala bears, or busy as beavers?

Put a check by the characteristics that describe you, a co-worker, or customer. It is common to have traits of several animals, but usually one or two areas are dominant.

The Law Abider

Animal: owl
Professions: police, accountants

- Quiet
- Reserved

- Interested in security
- Loyal
- Faithful
- Dependable, on time
- Believes in laws and traditions
- Honest
- Stressed with moving "out of the box"
- Prefers coloring within the lines

The Protector

Animal: wolf
Professions: news providers, social workers

- Literal
- Deals with concrete facts and needs
- Lives in the present
- Desires organization
- Honors traditions and beliefs
- Values competence and efficiency
- Takes charge
- Clear vision of what should be
- Can be critical and demanding
- More interested in self-evaluation than what others think

The Caregiver

Animal: Labrador retriever
Professions: ministry, teachers

- Warmhearted and kind
- Believes the best in people
- Exceptional memory for details that are important to their value system
- Reads body language
- Values security and kindness
- Respects traditions and laws
- Strong sense of duty
- Sense of balance
- Empathetic

The Technician

Animal: beaver
Professions: engineers, scientists, financial analysts, statisticians

- Wants to understand why and how
- Logical analysis
- Practical concerns
- Adventuresome spirit
- Wants to do his own thing
- Desires fairness
- Enjoys being alone
- Lots of natural ability
- Trusts her instincts
- Inventive

The Doer

Animal: bee
Professions: ministry, teachers, politicians

- Wants to get on with it if something needs to be done
- Straight-shooting types who abide by the job description
- Blunt
- Judges priorities on long-term goals
- Fast-moving, fast-talking
- Bored if project is not in their interest
- Practical
- Enthusiastic
- Moves the job to completion

The Performer

Animal: otter
Professions: entertainers, sports

- Extreme interest in external evaluations
- Loves people
- Lively, fun, enjoys being the center of attention
- Decisions based on internal values
- Lives in the here and now
- Spontaneous
- Becomes depressed and overwhelmed by stress or by being alone
- Keen appreciation for aesthetics
- Rules are guidelines

- More interested in working together and getting everyone on board than the final product

The Artist

Animal: Siamese cat
Professions: authors, artists, zookeepers

- Focus is self and feelings
- Keenly in touch with senses: look, feel, taste, sound, smell
- Quiet and reserved, difficult to get to know
- Animal and nature lover
- Likes hands-on, simple
- Extremely perceptive and aware of others
- Warm and sympathetic
- No desire to be a leader
- Perfectionist traits
- Not willing to flit from project to project until all effort has been expended on current concept

The Executive

Animal: elephant
Professions: business, politics, leadership

- Enjoys leading
- Bulldozer
- Dominates and controls
- Not detail oriented
- No patience for inefficiency

- Not particularly caring for other's feelings
- Strong sense of confidence
- Forceful and decisive
- Does not deal well with feelings and values
- Strong critic of the status quo
- Believes the ends justify the means

The Visionary

Animal: lion
Professions: politics, professors

- Dominant leader
- Intuitive
- Very aware of all aspects of culture
- Enthusiastic about their ideas
- Fluent conversationalist and loves debate
- Mentally quick
- Values knowledge and one's own evaluation of information
- Charismatic
- Likes to assign the workload

Appendix 2

The Workplace Stress Barometer

Every workplace has stress. Think about your current job and rate how often each of the following statements describes your feelings. It will be clear whether you need to find ways to ameliorate the stress by adjusting your schedule, counseling, developing better coping skills, changing positions within the company to find a better fit, or possibly seeking other employment.

Most of us have some parts of our job that are not enjoyable. However, if you answer "very often" to even half of the statements, you need to act to bring healthy change to lessen your negative feelings. Your goal is to find ways to use your gifts and talents within your current job, if possible. Talk through your issues with someone who has the power to bring about change. Adjust your attitude if issues are irresolvable and you feel you have no alternative to your current job. Allowing issues to simmer and your stress barometer to rise is a no-win for you and your employer.

Consider yourself fortunate if you have a score, when tallied, of 38 or less. The closer you move from 38 to 50, the more you must evaluate whether the problem is you, your self-esteem, or your company culture. Work toward resolution. You don't want to be like the frog who stayed too long in hot water.

Question	Never	Rarely	Sometimes	Often	Very Often
1. I feel under tension from the moment I walk in the door at work until I leave.	1	2	3	4	5
2. I worry about how I am perceived at work.	1	2	3	4	5
3. I have too much work to do in a reasonable time frame.	1	2	3	4	5
4. My responsibilities at work are causing tension in my personal life.	1	2	3	4	5
5. I feel unable to control what is expected of me.	1	2	3	4	5
6. I do not feel I am using my gifts and talents.	1	2	3	4	5
7. I feel unappreciated.	1	2	3	4	5
8. I feel uncomfortable expressing my concerns or ideas.	1	2	3	4	5
9. I am unable to say no.	1	2	3	4	5
10. I fantasize about having a different job.	1	2	3	4	5

Notes

Chapter 2 Who Is the Problem?

1. Harris Interactive, "Attitudes in the American Workplace VII, The Seventh Annual Labor Day Survey," Marlin Company telephone polling, May/June 2001.

Chapter 5 My Behavior—My Choice?

1. *Shrek*, directed by Andrew Adamson and Vicky Jenson (DreamWorks, 2001), DVD.

2. Bureau of Economic Analysis, "Employer Costs for Employee Compensation," March 9, 2011, http://www.bea.gov.

3. Ibid.

4. Adapted from Elizabeth B. Brown, *Living Successfully with Screwed-Up People* (Grand Rapids: Revell, 1999), 38–39.

Chapter 6 People Don't Want to Be Fixed

1. National Institute of Mental Health, "How Common is ASD?" accessed December 5, 2011, http://www.NIMH.nih.gov/health/publications/a-parents-guide-to-autism-spectrum-disorder/how-common-is-asd.shtml.

2. March Hausey, "Heroes—Temple Grandin," *Time*, April 29, 2010.

3. Claudia Wallis, "Temple Grandin on Temple Grandin," *Time*, February 4, 2010.

Chapter 7 Is This Job Right for You?

1. Lawrence M. Miller, *Barbarians to Bureaucrats: Corporate Life Cycle Strategies* (New York: Clarkson N. Potter, 1989).

2. Geoff Colvin, "Steve Jobs' Bad Bet," *Fortune*, March 19, 2007.

Chapter 9 The Generation Problem

1. Jessica Stollings Strang, personal interview, August 2010, Jessica@re-gen erations.org.
2. Karl Fish and Scott McLeod, PhD, *Did You Know 2.0*, Colorado Springs, CO, September 2009, http://www.youtube.com/watch?v=6ILQrUrEWe8.

Chapter 10 Minding the Family Store

1. Stacy Perman, "Taking the Pulse of Family Business," *Bloomberg News-week*, February 13, 2006, http://www.businessweek.com/smallbiz/content/feb2006/sb20060210_476491.htm.
2. "Start-up Statistics," http://www.247advisor.com/artman/publish/start-up-statistics.html.
3. "Edsel B. Ford," http://www.edsel.com/pages/edslford.htm.
4. Ibid.
5. K. Alderson, "Women Taking Leadership Role In Family Business," *Focus*, National Association of Women Business Owners (NAWBO), 2011.
6. William T. O'Hara, *Centuries of Success: Lessons from the World's Enduring Family Businesses* (Avon, MA: Adams Media Corp., 2003).
7. "Family Quotations," BrainyQuote, http:///www.brainyquote.com/quotes/keywords/family.html.

Chapter 11 Held Hostage by Manipulation

1. Martin Kantor, *The Psychopathology of Everyday Life* (Westport, CT: Praeger, 2006), 43–44.

Chapter 13 Building Stress Absorbers into Your Life

1. Beth Azar, "A New Take on Psychoneuroimmunology," *Monitor on Psychology* 32, no. 11 (December 2001): 34.
2. David Larson, MD, *General Hospital Psychiatry* 11, no. 5 (September 1989): 345–51.
3. J. J. Lynch, *The Language of the Heart: The Body's Response to Human Dialogue* (New York: Basic Books, 1985).
4. American Institute of Stress, "Is There a Simple but Accurate Way to Measure Stress?" http://www.stress.org/scoop-IS-THERE-A-SIMPLE-BUT-ACCURATE-WAY-TO-MEASURE-STRESS--269.htm, 2011.
5. American Institute of Stress, "Job Stress," www.stress.org/job.htm.
6. Lynch, *Language of the Heart*, 45.
7. Malcolm Gladwell, *The Outliers* (New York: Little, Brown & Co., 2008).
8. "14.2 'The Roseto Effect,'" http://www.uic.edu/classes/osci/osci590/14_2%20The%20Roseto%20Effect.htm.
9. C. Shaffer and K. Anundsen, "The Healing Powers of Community," *Utne Reader*, September–October, 1995.
10. For a comparison of Roseto Valfortore, Italy, and Roseto, Pennsylvania, see Carla Bianco, *The Two Rosetos* (Bloomington: Indiana University Press, 1974).

11. Grossman and Leroux, "A New Roseto Effect," *Chicago Tribune*, October 11, 1996.

12. "Retiring at 55 Increases Death Risk in New Study," http://www.senior journal.com/NEWS/Retirement/5-10-21Retire55.htm.

13. Robert O'Brien, *Marriott: The J. W. Marriott Story* (Salt Lake City: Desert Book Co., 1977).

Chapter 14 When Dealing with Emotions, Do the Outrageous

1. Elizabeth B. Brown, *The Joy Choice* (Grand Rapids: Revell, 1995), 73–76.

2. Rajwin Singh, "Interview with Rick Warren by Paul Bradshaw," *South Asian Connection*, March 28, 2005, http://www.southasianconnection.com/blogs/18/ Interview-with-Rick-Warren-by-Paul-Bradshaw.

3. http://www.answers.com/topic/this-too-shall-pass-1#cite_note-Keyes160-0.

Chapter 15 Let It Go

1. Brown, *Living Successfully with Screwed-Up People*, 159–60.

Chapter 17 Touch with Words

1. Stephen Covey, *The Seven Habits of Highly Effective People: Powerful Lessons in Personal Change* (London: Simon & Schuster, 2004), 204.

2. Jon Spoelstra, *Marketing Outrageously Redux: How to Increase Your Revenue by Staggering Amounts* (Austin: Bard Press, 2008), 51.

3. Daniel Kurtzman, "Ronald Reagan Quotes," http://politicalhumor.about. com/cs/quotethis/a/reaganquotes.htm.

4. Brown, *Living Successfully with Screwed-Up People*, 38–39.

5. Covey, *Seven Habits of Highly Effective People*, 222.

6. Ronald C. Hamby, MD, FRCP, Alzheimer's Conference, March 2011, Quillen Medical School, Johnson City, TN.

Chapter 18 Are You as Wise as a Donkey?

1. "Learning Who Is Your Mother: The Behavior of Imprinting," http://www. cerebromente.org.br/n14/experimento/lorenz/index-lorenz.html.

2. Hanna Rosin, "The End of Men," *The Atlantic,* July/August 2010, http:// www.theatlantic.com/magazine/archive/2010/07/the-end-of-men/8135/.

3. U.S. Equal Employment Opportunity Commission, "New Gallup Poll on Employment Discrimination Shows Progress, Problems 40 Years After Founding of EEOC," December 8, 2005, http://www.eeoc.gov/eeoc/newsroom/release/12-8-05.cfm.

Chapter 19 The Tug-of-War

1. Randall S. Hansen, "Is Your Life in Balance? Work/Life Balance Quiz," *Quintessential Careers*, http://www.quintcareers.com/work-life_balance_quiz.html.

2. Bureau of Labor and Statistics, "Exploring Career Information," http:// www.bls.gov/.

3. Ellen Galinsky, "*Washington Post* Live Chat on Work Life Balance," Monday, August 18, 2010; 11:00 a.m.

Chapter 20 Love It or Leave It: A Crossroads Decision

1. Catherine Rampell, "Reader Response: How Many People Are Quitting Their Jobs?" *New York Times*, April 3, 2009, http://economix.blogs.nytimes.com/2009/04/03/reader-response-how-many-people-are-quitting/.
2. G. Aubrey Lee, "Health Care Debate Needs a 'Face,' not Political Gamesmanship," *Johnson City Press*, December 24, 2009, 8A.

Chapter 21 Handicapped, but Not Crippled

1. Spoelstra, *Marketing Outrageously Redux*, 51.
2. For more information on Dick and Rick Hoyt, including their complete race history, visit http://www.teamhoyt.com/.
3. "Mother Teresa: 'Do It Anyway,'" http://www.prayerfoundation.org/mother_teresa_do_it_anyway.htm.

Chapter 22 Answering the Questions

1. Robert Brault, http://www.robertbrault.com/2009/10/daily-quotes-1-through-7.html.
2. Vivian Komori, http://www.quotegarden.com/perseverance.html.

Elizabeth B. Brown received her bachelor's degree from Emory and Henry College and her master's degree in psychology and counseling from Virginia Commonwealth University. Betty is a frequent speaker for grief seminars, conferences, and women's religious retreats across the country, including Hospice, Contact, Christian Women's Club, Widowed Persons Association, and Compassionate Friends. She currently teaches a course on death and dying at East Tennessee State University Quillen Medical School. She and her physician husband, Paul, live in Johnson City, Tennessee.

A Bestseller That Continues to Change Lives and Relationships

You can succeed at work—no matter who you have to work with!

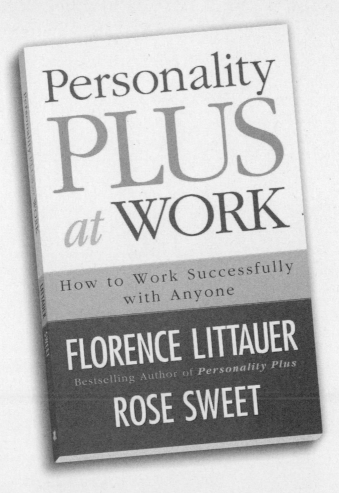

Did you know that you hold the key to working well with *all* of your co-workers? It comes from discovering how to harness the power of personality. Personality experts Florence Littauer and Rose Sweet show you how.

Revell
a division of Baker Publishing Group
www.RevellBooks.com

Available wherever books are sold.

You can have an organized office space
at work and at home.

This upbeat must-read will help you create
a personalized system that works for you.